OUT IN FRON

Out in Front

GEORGE GRETTON

PELHAM BOOKS

First published in Great Britain by
PELHAM BOOKS LTD
26 *Bloomsbury Street*
*London, W.C.*1
1968

© 1968 *by George Gretton*

Set and printed in Great Britain by
Tonbridge Printers Ltd, Peach Hall Works, Tonbridge, Kent
in Times ten on twelve point, and bound by
James Burn at Esher, Surrey

CONTENTS

ILLUSTRATIONS

The photograph of Alfred Shrubb facing page 33 is reproduced by courtesy of the *Radio Times and Hulton Picture Library*.

Foreword

In this book I have tried to humanise athletics: that is, to offer
something from my own knowledge to people who also know a
lot about running, but also to the discerning reader who does not,
but is interested in social history. Many books about athletics are
of their nature technical and statistical, produced by specialists for
students. These fulfil an important function, but are often esoteric.
I am trying to convey something of the humanity and glamour of
athletic competition to people who may never have thought of trying to run three miles in under 15 minutes (much less, as Ron
Clarke has done it, in under 13 minutes) but who can appreciate
the excitement and the aesthetic and social values of this most
austere and most colourful form of sport.

By an odd set of coincidences (some contrived) I have been
privileged to know in some degree most of the really outstanding
long-distance runners of modern times personally, right back to
the first of them, W. G. George, who was born well over a century ago. I never saw him run, but he was a friend of my father
and sometimes talked to me (without any condescension) and even
gave me a penny – which was a lot of money in those days when
delicious sweets could be bought at four ounces a penny.

Alfred Shrubb was a more difficult man to know, but he was a
legend in my youth and it was exciting to find him installed as
coach at Oxford when I went there and joined the OUAC. I
met Nurmi four times, twice in competition, and managed each
time to talk to him rather briefly: I doubt if anyone ever had a
really discursive conversation with Nurmi.

The others whom I have discussed in detail, Zatopek, Chataway
and Ron Clarke, have all taken time off from active lives to talk
athletics to me, and I am immensely grateful to them. The last

9

one, Abebe Bikila, whom I have never met in the flesh, I owe to an Ethiopian friend, Berhanu Tibebu, of the *Ethiopian Herald*, who conducted a special interview with him at my request and has given me permission to publish his report.

I am also indebted to that distinguished athlete and writer on athletics, Harold Abrahams, for patiently handing out information and allowing me to consult his unique library on athletics. The *News of the World*, which has done so much to encourage athletics in this country, especially by its sponsorship of the British Games, has kindly supplied me with the text of the obituary article on W. G. George, by the late Joe Binks, which it published in 1943.

I have been deeply impressed and moved by the disinterested help I have had – just for the asking – from many sources in many countries. It is easy to say that Olympic and other officials are obsolete or pompous (some of them are) but such faults and the occasional frictions of international competition, weighed against the immense positivity of athletics as a meeting-point, are marginal.

My own running achievement, against the rich background of the athletes I have known and written about, was not substantial, but it went far enough to give me an insight into what the performances of people like Nurmi, Zatopek, Chataway, Clarke or Bikila really meant. That and my interest in social history – which means what people are and have been like – is my excuse for writing a book about running, which I hope will give some pleasure to athletes and non-athletes. Actually, no excuse is really needed, because athletics is a fascinating subject in its own right. If I have failed to convey that fascination, it is not because I was once an indifferent runner, but am now an indifferent writer.

In looking at the perspective of athletic competition, I have been struck by the persistence with which certain factors and problems have recurred, from Classical Greece to modern Europe and America. I have dealt with certain points more than once, in different contexts. If this seems repetitious, it is because I thought it better to risk that rather than failing to communicate by being elliptical.

This book does not concern the Olympic Games as such, only their influence on the development of long-distance running. I have, however, provided in an Appendix some basic facts about Olympic competition which may help non-specialist readers to understand more easily the reports they will read from Mexico

City in October 1968. Where the Olympics most concern running at the moment is in the highly controversial decision to hold these Games in Mexico City at a height of over 7,000 feet. This is discussed in Chapter III.

No one doubts that the Mexicans will provide excellent facilities and overwhelming hospitality, but the decision is a new departure in two ways: the Games have never before been held at an altitude appreciably above sea level, and they have always been held in industrially advanced countries. Both these habits had to be broken some time. The less advanced nations are bound to want to play their part in the responsibility for such an imaginative undertaking as the Olympic Games have become, and especially considering they stand to gain advantage precisely in the economic field where their weakness lies, there is every reason why they should. Again, the problems arising from high-altitude competition had to be faced some time, and we have already learned a great deal from the preliminary trials and experiments.

Some athletes will be at a disadvantage, but they are mostly not the sort of people who complain about their luck. What does arise is a great opportunity to face up to implications of this new development, and particularly for all those who care about athletics and fair competition to put pressure on their National Associations, and through them on the Olympic Committee, to take the amateur definition out of its moth-balls, blow away the dust, and bring it up to date.

1
The Origins

Every fourth year, the world-wide interest in athletics – running, jumping and throwing things – rises to a chronic crescendo with the approach of a new Olympiad. Olympic programmes become more and more over-crowded with team-contests, but most of these are side-shows. Some, like football, are not of world class owing to the rules about amateur status; others, like ice-hockey or basket-ball, are not universal sports. The heart of the matter is in the running and the field events, and there is a special fascination about the middle and longer distance races.

Sprints, jumps and throwing are explosive events, where the actual performance is the tip of the iceberg and the real accomplishment is the technical perfection and concentration which enable the performer to deploy his energy in the precise form and at the precise moment which give the explosion its maximum effect. Once the jumper's foot has left the take-off or the discus-thrower is in his final swing, there is little more he can do about it: the result – and its appreciation – will depend on the elaborate series of movements which preceded the release, and the concentration with which they were carried out.

So the appreciation of explosive events, including sprinting, depends very much on a sophisticated understanding of the technique which precedes the climax, and the act is less exciting in human terms than the longer-distance race in which athletes are seen to be competing, with a combination of grace and endurance, for 4, 13 or 27 minutes at a stretch, with the result perhaps remaining in doubt until the final seconds. The pole-vaulter may have exerted as much energy and concentration spread over two hours as the three-miler in about 13 consecutive minutes, but the watcher can more easily participate in the three-miler's effort, because it is spread out continuously before his eyes, and the competitive element is clearly seen from first to last.

There are other factors in audience participation: flight and the chase are associated with the primordial instincts of self-preservation and never fail to stir the emotions. Any film director knows that there is nothing like a good chase for a climax to a thriller. The aesthetic pleasure is prolonged by continuity. The discus-thrower achieves a moment of superb grace at his last turn, but it is a moment – a still, not a movie. This can be captured, as Myron did it, and a good snapshot can freeze the statuesque moment of any explosive event – the pole-vaulter on his final kick, the sprinter coming out of his holes – but it cannot convey the fluent beauty of the runner. The nearest thing to a half-dozen runners seen moving rhythmically in line along the back straight is in a Greek frieze, such as the charioteer of Scopas, but the fluency can only be hinted at. The reality is always more exciting. The Renée Sintenis bronze of Paavo Nurmi which was so much admired in the 1930s is beautiful, but it is not Nurmi in action.

Then again, the spectacle of athletes enduring to their limit touches something very deep in human moral consciousness. They are competing against each other, but they are also competing with the limits set by the physical nature of the Universe: time, space and gravity, and the unforgiving minute, and in doing so they raise human stature.

The question is often asked: 'Why do they do it?' Sometimes facetiously ('Couldn't you catch a bus?') sometimes in puzzlement, sometimes in awe, but always with an underlying sense of respect. Before we try to answer this question, let us consider what athletics is today and how it has grown.

Athletics is a Greek word (ATHLOS – contest; ATHLON – prize) and athletics as we know it is a Greek concept: a contest for a prize. Bound up with it was quite early on, the concept of professionalism – the competition and the prize, in money or kind. In other ancient civilisations, Cretan, Persian, Chinese, there were sports and games, but it was in Greece that the competitive spirit was developed, for better or worse, at an early stage. Competition was already there in Homer's time.

Homer is now generally agreed to have written his Iliad or

Odyssey (or both) round about 800 BC, when Greek athletic competitions of the Olympic type were already established. He was using oral traditional material (much of it passed on in verse form) from a much earlier society – around 1100 BC. The athletic contests he describes, such as the funeral games laid on by Achilles for Patroclus in the Iliad (XXIII) and the hospitable sports-meeting laid on by Alcinous, King of the Phaeacians, for Ulysses in the Odyssey (VIII), are supposed to have happened two or three centuries before Homer was born, but they are reported so vividly that they must have reflected the form in Homer's own time. In the foot-race in the Iliad, for instance, (for which the first prize was a wine-mixing bowl of chased silver, holding 6 pints) Ajax was the front-runner, and Odysseus followed him 'close as the girdled woman brings the shuttle to her breast as she carefully draws it along to get the bobbin past the warp. So little was there in it. Odysseus's feet were falling in the tracks of Ajax before the dust had settled down again; and on the back of his head, Ajax felt the breath of the hero, who ran lightly and relentlessly on.'

The Homeric simile has become a cliché, but only because Homer wrote so long ago and has had so many imitators. In the original, it was always drawn from observation, and so this description of a front-runner with somebody breathing down his neck must have been. The incident might well have happened in the heroic era which Homer described from hearsay, but the terms of the description are contemporary, that is, they describe running when the Greek athletics we understand as classical were already organised. By the 8th Century, BC, the Olympiad, the Sports at Olympia, was firmly established and continued to be held every fourth year from then until the year 393 AD, an unbroken sequence of nearly twelve centuries.

The Cretans had developed many forms of sport before about 2000 BC. Bull-fighting (mostly unarmed combat of the Wild West rodeo type) boxing, wrestling, gymnastics, throwing events and the ball-game, were widely practised and enjoyed as spectacles. The Chinese played some sort of football several centuries before the Christian era and they did a great deal of boxing and wrestling: they taught the Japanese Judo, which developed to Karate. All these forms of sport evolved from hunting, military exercises, or religious cults, and their object was either military training, ritual or mere amusement for those taking part or those watching.

The Greek development of athletics was more complex. One element was certainly military training: the Greeks were seldom at peace, and local wars had to be fought often at short notice, so that the average citizen's freedom and survival rate depended on his physical fitness. The pursuit of athletics, especially running and throwing, was thus an essential part of education and citizenship, but, in order to sustain interest in these exercises, the Greeks organised competitions which, as the City States developed, became inter-city and international.

The Olympic festival began as a religious occasion centred on the temple of Zeus, to celebrate a victory and offer thanksgiving for peace. This is fully in line with the heroic tradition which Homer describes: any important occasion, a wedding, a funeral, a victory or the assembly of an army to go to war: any of these events, as we know from even a cursory study of the Homeric poems, was regarded as a good enough reason for throwing a party, with a sports meeting, prizes, sacrifices to the gods, and an enjoyable feast at which the sacrificial victims (and some of the prizes) were consumed with gusto.*

This is in line with the ethos of any warlike, aristocratic society, as for instance in the early Middle Ages, where Anglo-Saxons did their martial exercises and hoped that 'men would speak well of them after they were dead'. Much of medieval literature consisted of sagas and romances celebrating heroic deeds and feats of strength, as when Beowulf was alleged to have swum for 9 days and nights in the Baltic. But the Greeks had long before developed this cult of athletic excellence into a competitive system.

It is believed that the Games at Olympia, which had been discontinued, were re-started in 766 BC (perhaps within Homer's life-time) to mark a truce between two local kings, Cleosthenes of Pisa, and Iphitus of Elis. The truce was sanctified and its terms were inscribed on a bronze discus which still existed in the time of Pausanias, the geographer who wrote a travel book about Greece in the Second Century AD (called the PERIEGESIS = tour or swanning). The Games continued every fourth year from then till 393 AD: as though the present AAA Championships had been run uninterruptedly since the time of King Alfred.

This truce was a special one, stringently enforced on the

* One champion was said to have won a bull as a prize for weight-lifting, carried it round the Stadium and then eaten it himself in 24 hours.

authority of Zeus, and it had a strong influence on the character of the Olympic Games, which always marked an agreed respite from war. When the idea of the Games spread round the Greek world, the truce could last two or three months, while envoys with diplomatic immunity travelled round to announce the Games, and competitors were given safe-conduct. The effect of the Olympic Games was therefore to suspend local wars for a sizeable period. They also became a powerful stimulus to nationalism, or Pan-hellenism. The Greeks were insidious colonists who founded City-states all round the Aegean, and in Asia Minor and Southern Italy. In the 6th Century BC other sports festivals grew up, of which three attained Pan-hellenic status, like the Olympics. They were at Delphi (the Pythian), Corinth (the Isthmian) and Nemea (the Nemean). Many local festivals with sports-meetings sprang up, but these four were national (or 'Commonwealth') and, occurring annually over the four-year cycle, did more than anything else – except the Greek language – to create a national ethos in this individualistic and contentious people.*

Athletics was a part of the Greek temperament and *Weltanschauung*. Greeks loved beauty, they admired physical fitness, they were extrovert egoists, and they were deeply superstitious. Athletic competition against a residual background of religious cults fulfilled all the needs of these qualities. The Greeks were not sportsmen in the contemporary, English sense of the word. The loser got no sympathy: the nub of the thing was to win. That was what competition was about, and the emphasis was on competition.

To the Greeks, athletics was simply competition for a prize. What we would now call athletics (the functions of running, jumping and throwing things or people) they described as gymnastics, which means literally exercising in the nude (gymnas–naked). This was logical, since the most popular sport, wrestling, was more efficiently done in the nude, so that, with the aid of olive oil, the wrestler was at his least vulnerable. It caused some heart-searching about women's athletics (or gymnastics). These were permitted (including wrestling) in Sparta, but not elsewhere in the full sense of the term. Plato, in his 'Laws' says that girls should be encouraged to run, but in appropriate clothing. This is the custom

* The four great athletic festivals were actually rather more than annual: the Olympic and Pythian were held every four years, but the Isthmian and Nemean were every two years, so that there was some overlapping.

B

in the world of today, and perhaps underlines the influence of
Plato and Aristotle on our thinking.

In the Olympic and other athletic festivals, the Greeks
developed the essentials of modern athletics: running, jumps,
discus, javelin, boxing, wrestling and the pankration (a form of
all-in wrestling in which only biting and gouging were barred) as
well as chariot-racing, horse-racing and the pentathlon – the prize
for five events. As time went on, longer races were introduced,
and there were also boys' and youths' events. At first the only
foot-race was the stade, i.e. the length of the stadium, which
varied locally from just under 200 yards to over 200 metres.
The stadium was narrow – about 30 yards wide – so that when
longer races were introduced they were almost straight-up-and-
down, the runners turning left about round a post and coming
straight back, without any benefit of bends. The *diaulos* (which
means double-pipe) was two stades, corresponding to the quarter-
mile, and the long-distance race, the *dolichos*, varied locally from
7 stades up to 24, which at Olympia would be about 3 miles.
There were no longer races than this: the marathon, as we shall
see later, was a purely modern invention, based on a legend that
one, Pheidippides, ran from Marathon to Athens after the battle
to bring the news. Another legend suggests that the run was made
by a deserter. Nor is there any reason to believe, as has sometimes been suggested, that the Greeks regarded running any more
highly than other events: boxing, wrestling and chariot-racing were
the most popular, but fleetness of foot (TACHYTAS PODŌN)
was always respected.

There is some confusion about the mechanics of the Greek
stadium. The greatest authority on Greek athletics, Ernest
Gardiner, assumed that in a *diaulos* (or quarter-mile) which was
two lengths of the stadium, the runners ran in lanes each to a
separate turning-post (KAMPTĒR), hared round it and back down
their lane. In 1956 a German scholar, Oscar Broneer, showed
from excavations at Isthmia that the posts (or their sockets) from
which Gardiner deduced his turning-posts were almost certainly a
form of starting gates (HUSPLEX) with arms like railway signals
which were released at the start (as nowadays with horses), and
that all the runners turned round one post, which was situated at
Olympia a little to the left of centre, in order not to give the
man in the centre lane too much advantage. This is clearly ex-

plained by H. A. Harris in his *Greek Athletes and Athletics*, Chapter IV.

The whole problem of starting and of rounding the turning-posts was considerable, and is reflected in frequent references in Greek literature. The edge of competition, just as it bred professionalism, also bred cheating. To 'beat the pistol' (which was in earlier Greek times a trumpet) was to gain an advantage in a competition which had strong financial implications, and this could have serious consequences. There are cases on record of a loser obtaining substantial damages in law against the judges. Until the development of the HUSPLEX (the mechanically operated starting-gate) discipline was enforced by physical punishment, and in earlier illustrations the starter is always shown with a long and vicious-looking stick, with which any runner who 'beat the trumpet' was mercilessly flogged. There is also evidence of cutting corners: in the free-for-all at the turning-post in a *diaulos*, it was often possible for a runner to swerve inside the post (screened by the great cloud of dust thrown up from the dirt-track) and gain a good second, or ten yards. Apart from the dust-screen, the judges at the turning posts (also armed with long sticks) were under the disadvantage that the naked athletes had nothing on which to pin a number, to identify them. Much obviously depended on the umpire's prompt and skilful use of his stick.

The great Greek contribution to athletics was in introducing the competitive element and in elevating athletics to a high aesthetic and social status. The 6th Century BC was the age of strong men who were admired for their prowess. There are many stories of great feats of strength, especially in weight-lifting, some of which are documented. A block of sandstone was found at Olympia weighing nearly 3 cwt. with a 6th Century inscription saying that BYBON threw it over his head with one hand. He presumably raised it like a modern weight-lifter and released it with a one-handed thrust. Another block, weighing about half a ton, was, according to its inscription, raised from the ground by Eumastas, the son of Critobulus. Neither feat is incredible by contemporary standards. This cult of strength is reflected in Greek art at the time, just as a century later (in the 5th Century BC) a less muscular and more graceful form is depicted, and after the 4th Century over-specialised physiques are shown which have lost the classical proportions. They represented the specialists in one field or another.

The Greeks also organised all the facilities for athletics and physical training: the gymnasium, with its trainers, baths, changing-rooms and so on. The gymnasium was actually a sports-ground with running track and other outdoor facilities for exercise in the nude. What we now call a gymnasium corresponds to the *palaestra*, a building for wrestling and other indoor exercises. The Greeks of the 5th Century despised barbarians for not cultivating athletics and not being prepared to compete in the nude, and they took a dim view of Greeks who did not keep their bodies in good trim. Top Greeks were athletic (and gymnastic).

This cult of physical fitness produced a society comparable with English public schools a generation ago, where all boys were expected to keep fit and play games, and those who did not were not well thought of: a predominantly male society with some homosexual tendencies. It also produced professionalism.

The cult of athletic success bred specialisation, and a class of people concentrating on performance. The competition at inter-city or inter-state level became more and more intense, with corresponding partisanship. To win an event in one of the Pan-hellenic Games conferred enormous prestige on a city, and great *kudos* on the individual winner, as in modern international competition. The official prize was always honorary: an olive-wreath at Olympia, cut from the sacred tree behind the Temple of Zeus, a crown of bay-leaves at Delphi, a wreath of pine-leaves at Corinth, and parsley at Nemea. But, as in modern times, the State for whom the honour was gained treated the champion as a VIP, and the fringe benefits were substantial. Athens in the time of Solon paid 500 drachmae to any gold medallist (or olive-wreather) at Olympia, and his other privileges included a front seat at all public festivals, free meals and even tax-exemption.

Moreover, at the innumerable city-festivals which did not have Pan-hellenic status, prizes of substantial monetary value were offered. Some cities paid athletes from elsewhere to represent them. There was already something like the system of buying players in twentieth century football: but the players got the big end of the transfer, not the Clubs.

With such inducements, it is not surprising that a class of professional athletes grew up, travelling from meeting to meeting, seeking prizes and fringe benefits. This meant that standards of performances continually rose and specialisation resulted. New systems of training and diet were introduced, and athletics became a full-time occupation. The earlier ideal of all-round physical development was lost, so that athletics fell into disrepute. In Athens especially, young gentlemen no longer practised physical training. They found their sporting diversions in horse-racing or quail-fighting, and left the dust and heat of the stadium to the paid performers.

Serious Greek writers constantly condemned this development. Eurypides said of athletes: 'In youth they strut about in splendour, the idols of the city, but when bitter old age comes on them they are cast aside like worn-out cloaks'.*

A. E. Housman's poem 'To an Athlete Dying Young' is set ostensibly in a Shropshire town, but like most of his work, it has a Greek background:

> 'Now you will not swell the rout
> Of lads who wore their honours out,
> Runners whom renown outran,
> And the name died before the man.'†

A chap (or lad) in a Shropshire town who had really won distinction at running would not really, as Housman suggests, be happy to die young. He would be far more likely to end his days being listened to respectfully in the local pub (or even managing it). In Olympic Greece there was no such sentiment. He was out as soon as he had failed to win his last race.

The Athletics festivals continued for many centuries in their professional form, in which specialists had the edge – although old-time amateurs sometimes entered and even won in the pentathlon, in which the specialised professionals lost their advantage (just as an amateur rider sometimes comes up in the Grand National).

When the Romans took over the Greek world, for all administrative purposes, professional athletics survived, but were finally engulfed in the world of *circenses* – the spectacular circuses which made the masses forget their wrongs in chariot-races and vicarious blood-sports.

* Autolycus (fragment c. 440 BC).
† *A Shropshire Lad*, 1896.

There was no organised athletic competition in the Dark Ages which followed the fall of the Roman Empire. The Germanic civilisations were martial and aristocratic in the Homeric sense. There was constant physical training of one kind or another for the endemic wars, and there were pleasures which included spontaneous competition in leaping, running and jumping, but, when in the Middle Ages the feudal system was established, equitation became the sport of gentlemen. The legendary King Arthur, around whom so much medieval literature was written, was almost certainly a Roman-British military leader who halted the progress of the invading Germanic hordes at the beginning of the 6th Century by organising cavalry. The Romans had learned to their cost at the battle of Adrianople in 378, where they were cut up by the Visigoths and their Emperor Valens was killed, that heavy cavalry would always defeat infantry. This lesson was almost the last one they learnt and passed on to their successors. It was applied by Arthur, Artorius, or whatever his name may have been, when he defeated the Saxon invaders who fought on foot, but the Roman-Britons were eventually swamped by weight of numbers, and the Saxons never learned the strategical importance of cavalry. If they had, neither the Viking invasions of the 9th and 10th Centuries, nor the Norman Conquest could have succeeded.

After 1066, horsemanship was imported from the Continent and for many centuries the sport of gentlemen was centred on horses. Nevertheless, the common people (as excluded from Magna Carta) continued to find pleasure in athletic sports, leaping, running, throwing and wrestling, as the Greeks had done more than two thousand years before. Long-jumping was a prevalent sport, associated with leaping brooks and other natural obstacles. In the fen country, pole-vaulting was used for this purpose very early. Village sports and games persisted and flourished, and prowess at running, jumping and throwing was esteemed. Henry VIII was alleged to be an outstanding athlete, and probably was. It is possible that some of his opponents, for reasons of State, pulled their punches or shortened their strides, but the important thing is that this rather Gaulliste monarch, who wanted to be both despotic and popular, should have obviously enjoyed athletics and should have thought it worthwhile to build athletic ability into the image of the new Tudor dynasty. This reflects a strong popular participation in athletics which would respond to the image of Bluff King Hal out-running, out-jumping and out-throwing his subjects, when he was not composing lyrics, or re-marrying.

The popular interest in all forms of sport is constantly reflected in Elizabethan literature, as is the upper-class devotion to hunting and the other equestrian sports, with their Norman-French vocabularies. But even in Shakespeare's time the new spirit of puritanism was gaining ground, and won ascendancy in the 17th Century. It did not approve of sport, whether on foot or on horse-back.

The Puritans discouraged sports on Sundays and the traditional festivals which led to gambling and what they considered orgies of dancing, feasting and drinking, with a good deal of sexual promiscuity.

The condition of roads in the 17th Century may appear irrelevant to track records set up by Nurmi, Zatopek or Clarke, but there is a tenuous connexion. When the Puritans, generally well controlled by that great Statesman, Oliver Cromwell, came into power after the Civil War of 1642–46, many gentlemen in the South of England who had supported the Crown against Parliament retired to country estates in Essex, Kent, Hampshire, Sussex, Suffolk and so on. Being excluded from politics and cultural life, which were both in Puritan keeping, they concentrated on sporting activities. This was the period when cricket, played on the estates of the landed gentry, developed into at least the embryo of its present (or perhaps recent) form. The wicket grew out of the stool (when cricket was stool-ball) and became stabilised as a prototype of what bowlers aim at today. It is true that the bat continued to look like a hockey-stick until over 100 years later. But the foundations of cricket, as we now understand it, were laid in that period.

Here we are concerned not with cricket but with running. But it is also relevant that the opting out of gentlemen on the losing side in the Civil War to their country estates also extended the cultural boundaries of London as much as 60 miles in several directions. There had in the medieval past been powerful landowners who had defied the Crown, sometimes successfully. But, either they deposed the King, or the King disposed of them. In the 17th Century a more urbane process took place after the defeat and suspension (or decapitation) of the Crown. The losing faction simply spent more of their time on their country estates, or in some cases built themselves houses in the home counties (there are many beautiful 17th Century houses in Essex which owe their existence to the Civil War). This applied not to the nobility who had their country seats already, but to the 'mob of gentlemen who wrote with ease' in and around the court of Charles I. This was the first, rudimentary stage in the process by which South-Eastern England has become over-populated. After the Restoration many of these gentlemen remained for much of the year on their estates, and the defeat of Puritanism gave a new impetus to merry-making and country sports. The gentlemen had also become more mobile.

It was in this period that the gentry, who were doing a great deal more coach-travelling, employed footmen who really were footmen and not decorative young men for opening the front door. They operated private postal services and accompanied coaches on foot. On long journeys they ran on ahead of the coach to arrange for accommodation for the family when it arrived at an inn or at its destination. So they were chosen for their fleetness of foot and the practice grew up of their masters matching them against each other for wagers. It is recorded in the Diary of Sir Erasmus Phillips that in 1720 a foot-race around Woodstock Park was arranged between Grove (the Duke of Wharton's running footman) and Phillips (Mr Diston's). Sir Erasmus writes: 'My namesake ran the four miles course in 18 minutes and won the race, and thereby his master £1,000,' and he adds that there was 'a most prodigious concourse of people'.

Either the watch or the measurement of the course must have been wrong, as Ron Clarke could not have matched the recorded performance over rough ground wearing leather shoes and knee-breeches, but the incident illustrates the trend. For some reason, four miles became a popular distance* and this was reflected in the organised championship competitions in the 19th Century: the 3 and 6 miles races, corresponding to the Olympic distances, were not introduced into the AAA championships until 1932. Up to then the 4 miles was the main distance event. There was obviously great public interest in foot-racing, and gentlemen were prepared to bet large sums. So running took its place beside prize-fighting and a bit above wrestling as a sport which could attract spec-

* Perhaps because it was the circumference of an average park.

tators and prize-money, and the class of pedestrian (or ped) grew up with the pugilist (or pug).

At the same time, amateur running developed. The village sports was an integral part of country life, and the gentry participated in one way or another. Gentlemen also performed athletic feats themselves for wagers or to show what they could do, and this practice became very fashionable in the period of the Napoleonic wars, so much so that the first book on long-distance running* appeared in 1813, and is a mine of information on the exploits of the period, amateur and professional. There was, for instance, a lawyer's clerk, Foster Powell, who in 1764 ran 50 miles on the Bath Road in 7 hours, covering the first 10 miles in an hour, if the timekeepers and milestones can be trusted. He performed abroad in France and Switzerland, and later ran and walked from London to Canterbury and back in 24 hours (a distance of 122 miles). Long-distance feats of endurance aroused special interest. After Powell had twice travelled from London to York and back (over 400 miles) in less than 6 days, he was engaged to show his paces at Astley's Amphitheatre in London to packed houses.

Another celebrated pedestrian was Captain Barclay Allardyce, the special subject of Thom's book, and it is interesting that the pedestrians whose feats and competitions were recorded included not merely full-time professionals, but people from all walks of life – Army officers, country gentlemen, farmers, labourers, even a few butchers: although there was not then any systematic distinction between amateur and professional. A Mr Wallis of Jermyn St gave a foretaste of repetition-running by allegedly travelling 2 miles in 9 minutes in 2 'starts' with an interval of 1 minute between. Some fairly credible times are recorded of around 21 minutes for 4 miles, under 10 minutes for 2 miles and 10 miles in 57 minutes. Mile races were also run, mainly by 'Gentlemen', since the endurance tests attracted more attention and so yielded better returns for professionals. Times were of the order of 4 mins 50 secs, but in 1825 James Metcalf, described as the Champion, is reported to have run a mile in 4 mins 30 secs for a stake of 1,000 guineas. There were also sprint competitions and quarter-mile races.

Clocks and watches were quite accurate – John Harrison produced his first marine chronometer in 1730, and by 1800 the

* Pedestrianism, or an account of the Performance of Celebrated Pedestrians ... etc. by Walter Thom, Aberdeen 1813.

chronometer had been developed to its present form – but without stop-watches no event could be timed to seconds, and the measurement of courses and tracks was more traditional than scientific.

Army officers were particularly active in athletics and there was a possibility that organised amateur sport might have developed at Sandhurst in the 1820s, but the vogue of amateur sport receded for a decade or two and it was not till its revival in the forties that the permanent foundations of modern athletics were laid.

In the meantime, great changes had occurred in English education. There was a revival of learning after the complete slump in the 18th Century. Earnest dons at Oxford and Cambridge, and dynamic Public Schoolmasters were beginning to reflect the new spirit of reform and science. Organised games and athletics, combining manliness with intellectual vigour, were a part of this new trend. Older boys and undergraduates who had spent (or misspent) most of their time in dissipation were recalled to a more purposeful attitude to life which included a *mens sana in corpore sano*. Most people then still lived in or near the country – there were fields round Piccadilly and a dairy-farm in Soho – and boys used to enjoy the country sports in their holidays, but at school their games had not been organised. Thomas Gray, looking back on his schooldays at 18th Century Eton asks rhetorically:

> 'What idle progeny succeed
> To chase the rolling circle's speed,
> Or urge the flying ball?'

In the 1830s, however, partly because of the earlier vogue of pedestrianism, amateur and professional, schoolboys began competitive running. The steeplechase or cross-country run had a long tradition in country sports. Hunting was often done on foot – foxes, for instance, up to the 17th Century were hunted with beagles, and otter-hounds were also taken out on foot. A steeplechase was simply a race across country on foot or on horseback in which the steeples of churches were used as starting and finishing points because they were the obvious land-marks. Eton and Rugby had established regular annual cross-country competitions before 1840, and they and other schools were doing a good deal of running and jumping.

The take-off to the contemporary pattern of amateur athletic competition occurred in Oxford, where many of the pupils of the sports-minded schools had gone to study. The more affluent undergraduates did a good deal of riding, and Exeter College had for many years held a steeplechase race on horseback, usually called the 'College Grind'. After a disappointing race, some young gentleman complained of the quality of the hired horses, and the idea was thrown up of running a steeplechase on foot – a 'College foot-grind'. It was agreed to organise a 2 miles steeplechase together with some flat races from 60 yards to a mile, and a hurdle race of 140 yards over 10 flights of hurdles 10 yards apart. This was in 1850.

The meeting was organised facetiously as a sweepstake in which competitors were treated as horses and bets placed accordingly. A copy of the advertisement is preserved, which makes it clear that it was all conceived as an undergraduate joke – or a piece of horseplay – but it was a historic moment in athletics, and it is interesting that it occurred one year before the Great Exhibition at which Victorian England launched the consciousness of a new age of technological progress.

The periodical, *Bell's Life*, described this meeting and its successors as 'rural and interesting revels'. But within 5 or 6 years most Oxford and Cambridge Colleges had established organised sports meetings. Within 10 years there was inter-College competition, comparable with the inter-city Greek competitions, and 14 years later the first representative match between Oxford and Cambridge took place, and set the pattern of modern international competition in athletics. In the meantime, athletics had spread round schools and clubs in the country like a virus. The London Athletic Club began organising competitions in 1864 (although its name was assumed 2 years later). By then there were clubs and sports-meetings all over England, and the trend was spreading to the British colonies and the United States, which, as soon as it had settled its Civil War, moved over to a more urbane kind of conflict, and soon won great distinction.

2

Modern Competition

In 1866 the Amateur Athletic Club was formed and began to hold national championships at the Lillie Bridge ground in Fulham, but, although these were official, they were not representative, and there were crises to come.

An important element in the revival of athletics was dissociation from professional running which had fallen into disrepute – it is so much easier to 'nobble' humans than horses! The Oxford and Cambridge athletes who gave the great impetus to amateur athletics used a strict definition of amateur status which was in line with the 'Henley' definition for rowing. This did not recognise anyone as an amateur whose work involved strong physical effort (the 'mechanic, artisan and labourer class'). This was not entirely class distinction: a waterman who spent all his day at the oars would obviously have an advantage over an amateur oarsman, and the same might be argued of a blacksmith in weight-lifting or hammer-throwing, but it clearly makes no sense in running, and was not accepted in the North and Midlands.

The Amateur Athletic Club was formed mainly by Oxbridge athletes, and another bone of contention was that the championships were held soon after the Oxford and Cambridge Sports in the Spring, when other competitors had had no chance to train. Many athletes were all-rounders, playing football, cricket and even rowing: even in the nineties, C. B. Fry, the Long Jump world record-holder, was also an England cricketer and soccer player. So athletics was restricted to the Lent Term at the Universities.

In the North and Midlands, clubs accepted anyone as an amateur who did not actually run for money, and they took little interest in the Amateur Athletic Club meetings, which survived

28

for some years on the support of the London Athletic Club, to which many ex-Oxbridge athletes belonged. Matters came to a head in 1877, when the LAC moved to its own ground at Stamford Bridge and it was then said that the only active members of the AAC were the secretary, the pony and the roller.

There were actually three parties to the dispute: the AAC, the LAC and the provincial clubs. The Amateur Athletic Club was simply a projection of Oxford and Cambridge athletics. It was the clubs and their members at these two venerable universities which gave the impetus to the revival of organised athletic competition in the modern world, and athletics in Britain owes them a great debt. Their mistake was in trying, unconsciously, to mould all athletics in their own pattern.

The London Athletic Club was also a very gentlemanly affair. It was started in 1863 as the Mincing Lane Athletic Club and found a ground in South-West London, which is now the home of the Chelsea Football Club, Stamford Bridge. This area was chosen because 'it was near the stretch of the River Thames most suitable for rowing, and there was a connexion between rowing and running at that time. This was because of Oxbridge habits. The main sporting contests up to then had been cricket, rowing and football. No one specialised very seriously, and some really outstanding athletes were excellent in three or more disciplines. Most of them did a bit of everything, including polo. But there was a link between the two ball games, football and cricket, and a large number of players, amateur and professional, have reached international standard in both games. Cricket obviously had to be played in the summer term. Competitive football between the two Universities was played in the Michaelmas Term. In medieval tradition the Universities had three terms, the Michaelmas from October to December, the Lent from January to March, and the Hilary Term from April to June. Of these terms, the boatrace had claimed the middle one, and athletics had to fit in somewhere.

It went in with rowing in the middle term, partly because the ball-games players had an affinity, and usually played both games, and partly because runners and oarsmen had none at the higher level. They supplemented each other. Runners by rowing could build up strength (as they do nowadays by weight-lifting). Oarsmen could relieve their sedentary muscles and improve their performance by some gentle running, but no one could really be top class at both.

This was an excellent arrangement, but there was one snag. The Spring term, from January to March, is not the best time for athletics, for a number of reasons. One is that the optimum performance in running is achieved in warm climatic conditions, even in endurance events, and more so in 'explosive' ones. Another reason was that athletes everywhere except in Oxford and Cambridge were at a disadvantage in March. Even at the Stock Exchange, where not much manual work was done, it was not possible to get away for serious training before dark between January and March.

The AAC championships were held in the week after the Oxford-Cambridge Sports-meeting, when the University competitors had spent all their afternoons for two months training themselves to a peak of fitness. Other competitors had been restricted to week-ends. The same applied to clubs all over the country, where amateurs, whatever their social class, were not getting a fair crack of the whip if they had to compete at that time of year with the Varsity athletes.

The issue was forced by the London Athletic Club, when it boycotted the 1879 championships of the AAC, and organised a schismatic championship meeting of its own at Stamford Bridge in the summer. There was not much to choose between performances in the two opposition meetings. W. G. George turned out in the LAC meeting and won the mile and 4 miles. His mile performance was the fastest reliably recorded up to then, but his 4 miles was a little slower than that of the AAC winner. It was an obviously absurd situation, and the developing British athletic State was threatened with balkanisation. Some of the Midland clubs participated in the LAC summer championship, and one or two also made entries in the Spring AAC meeting. But the clubs in the North of England would have no part of it.

The feud threatened to run on. In the early Spring of 1880, before the University sports, the Amateur Athletic Club advertised another annual function as usual. With the London Athletic Club in opposition, and most clubs round the country tending to wish a plague on both houses, there was serious danger of disintegration.

That this was avoided was due largely to a group of athletes at Oxford, who were also men of intelligence. After the schism in 1879, and the threat of worse in 1880, the officers of the Oxford University Athletic Club persuaded the various dissident parties to attend a meeting in Oxford. This was a diplomatic initiative comparable with a United Nations peace-keeping mission over a frontier dispute, or the negotiation of demarcations between rival trade unions. The arbitrators wisely framed their invitation in the form of an afternoon meeting followed by dinner in that monument of Victorian Gothic, the Randolph, which then (as now) provided excellent food and drink. It is not a coincidence that three of the undergraduate officers of the Oxford University Athletic Club who initiated this move afterwards had distinguished legal careers. It seems a pity they did not go into the Diplomatic Service.

This was a decisive moment in the history of modern athletics, not merely in England. Out of it grew the Amateur Athletic Association which has since administered all amateur athletics in Britain and became the pattern for all the other countries round the world which organise athletic competition. Without this pattern, the Olympic Games could certainly not have been re-started in 1896.

The Amateur Athletic Association staged the first nation-wide championships in the summer of 1880, which have continued till now (war-years apart) and were from the first international, in that they were open to all comers. There are four degrees of records recognised in this competition: championship records, world records, British native records, and All-comers' records (which mean that anyone, from China to Peru, as long as he is an amateur, can be recognised as having put up the best performance ever in these islands). And of course he can win the AAA Championship and hold it as long as he can successfully defend it.

At the first meeting at Stamford Bridge in 1880 all the events, not surprisingly, were won by British competitors. But in 1881 an American, L. E. Myers, came over and won the 440 yards. American athletes continued to compete and, as time went on, Continental challengers appeared and often won, and Commonwealth athletes have long been prominent. The idea of universal international competition in the modern world dates from the renaissance of the Olympic Games in 1896, but long before that the AAA, created at that obscure meeting in Oxford in April

1880, had brought international competition into existence and continued to foster it.

It took some time for the Olympic Games to be established as the serious centre of world competition. The 1908 Games in London were a turning-point, and the Stockholm Games of 1912 were probably decisive in establishing the Olympic Games as the high point of world competition. But all this time, and for many years afterwards, the AAA championships were an annual focus of international competition. They were open to the best in the world – the 'all-comers' – and the first serious competition was from the European Games when they started in 1934.

Through the growth of these other international competitions, the AAA meeting has lost some of its status, but it continues to attract a considerable number of athletes from abroad. At the 1967 meeting, Ron Clarke successfully defended his 3 miles title, E. Burke of the United States won the hammer-throw, there was a large South African entry, both white and coloured, and a large entry from Continental countries on both sides of the Iron Curtain. Indeed, the Continental Athletic Associations agreed to use the AAA meeting as a selection trial for part of the team it was sending at short notice to Montreal for the match between Europe and the Americans. This was done partly because the date was convenient, but it was also a natural move, in view of the long international tradition of these championships.

At the Oxford meeting on April 24th, 1880, a set of resolutions drafted by the officers of the Oxford University Athletic Club, B. R. Wise, C. N. Jackson and Montague Shearman, were presented, aiming at creating a nation-wide body to control amateur athletics along clearly defined lines. The resolutions were a model of clarity and dealt with all the controversial points which had been bedevilling club relations. They were substantially adopted by the meeting which fully represented the main athletic interests of the country: the London and Amateur Athletic Clubs, the two University Clubs, the Midland and Northern Counties Associations, the leading Cross-country Clubs, the Civil Service Athletic Association (which was large and active) and several of the biggest and most active local clubs.* The objects of the Association were agreed to be:

* There is a full summary of the meeting's discussion in the AAA Jubilee Souvenir, *Fifty Years of Progress*, ed. H. F. Pash, 1931.

Above: Greek long distance runners. 333 BC. From a vase in the British Museum. *Below:* The Panathenaic Stadium at Athens, as restored for the first modern Olympic Games in 1896

Above: Ron Clarke (Australia) out in front, London 1966. *Below, left:* Alfred Shrubb, the first athlete in the modern tradition of systematic training. *Below, right:* W. G. George, who set a world professional Mile record of 4 min. 12¾ sec. in August 1885

1) To improve the management of athletics meetings and to promote uniformity of rules for the guidance of local committees;
2) To deal repressively with any abuses of athletic sports;
3) To hold an annual championship meeting.

The meeting also agreed on a definition of amateur status, which may not have been perfect, but was clear and practical, and it agreed that all races held under the sanction of the Association should be confined to amateurs, and that strict control should be exercised over the award of prizes, and certain practical steps should be taken to discourage the indiscriminate selling of prizes.

Then a committee of 10 members was elected to execute these resolutions and set up the Association. One of these, Lord Jersey, was elected President, and the three Oxford men, Wise, Jackson and Shearman, were elected as respectively Vice-President, Treasurer and Secretary.

Not long before then, Matthew Arnold had described Oxford as the 'home of lost causes and forsaken loyalties', but any Oxford man must be proud of that achievement. In the space of one day, numerous factions either antagonistic or neutralist were brought to a clear, precise agreement which they could accept on all the basic issues which had seemed insoluble. One cannot help feeling that if only the United Nations had had Messrs Wise, Jackson and Shearman to draft and explain their Charter (with as clear a definition of a threat to peace) the common man would have been saved enormous trouble and expense.

One shrewd proposal was that the National Championships should be held in rotation in London, the Midlands and the North. This arrangement did not actually last very long, but it did a great deal in that critical period to stop centrifugal impulses and reassure the provincial clubs that athletics would not in future be managed by a superior dog in London wagged by two tails in Oxford and Cambridge.

The definition of an amateur seems too narrow. In that very gentlemanly sport, cricket, amateurs played with professionals without contamination. But the AAA (which soon came to be called the Three A's) inherited a very different tradition. Pedestrianism until after 1850 was primarily a professional sport. The performers, from the running footmen onwards, who appeared in public, did it for money, and they were surrounded by bookmakers, who did not hesitate to cut corners by fixing results. This

C

sort of thing happens to this day in that sport of Kings, horse-racing. It was all too easy where the runner was a human being who could be persuaded for a consideration to let someone else win, and so upset the betting form to the advantage of those in the know.

Genuine, honest sport depends on keeping out this sort of corruption, and from this point of view there was a great deal of sense in the definition, accepted at the Oxford meeting, of an amateur as: 'Any person who has never competed for money, (or) with or against a professional for any prize, and who has never taught, pursued or assisted in the practice of athletic exercises as a means of obtaining a livelihood.'

This worked harshly a few years later against W. G. George, the first really great distance-runner in modern times, but it was necessary to stop athletics from being commercialised and corrupted. The process was not easy. The formation of the AAA coincided with a great wave of popular interest in running, which became the greatest draw to spectators wherever there were grounds large enough to accommodate them. This brought in spivs and dishonest book-makers and promoters.

Montague Shearman, one of the three Oxford men who stimulated the formation of the AAA (and afterwards became a Judge) wrote a book on athletics at the end of the century,* which is a most valuable document for the history of running in Victorian England, and in which he deals with the problems of professionalism very much as a Greek moralist might have done in the 5th Century BC. He says: 'A great many athletes who pass as amateurs are not only professionals in truth and fact, who make a living out of the sport, but, what is worse, many of them are making a living out of it by dishonest means.' He goes on to say: 'The latest abuse that has crept into amateur athletics is one which seems inevitably to follow every sport in which the presence of a well-known performer can be relied on to produce a large increase in the "gate-money" paid by the public. The best athletes, while passing as amateurs, earn the profits of a professional while touring throughout the country from ɔne meeting to another ... First, "travelling expenses" were allowed to the visiting celebrity; then "lump sums" for expenses; and, finally, the system sprang up of

---

* *Athletics*, by Montague Shearman, Longmans Green & Co., 1898, revised edition 1904.

the secretaries of clubs engaging so-called "amateurs" at a fixed
sum to perform at their meetings.'

In 1897 there was a scandal which caused half a dozen of the
worst offenders, most of them champions or record-holders, who
had spent every summer touring the country from meeting to
meeting, without visible means of support, to be expelled from
amateur competition.

Shearman went on to define very realistically the true functions
and limitations of the AAA. 'All a governing body of sport can
be expected to do is to keep order and punish offences against
its laws, and it can no more render its subjects good sportsmen
and amateurs than an Act of Parliament can render citizens vir-
tuous. What the AAA does for the true amateur is this: it assures
him that wherever he goes to run under AAA laws he will find
competent management and fair play – a fair field and no favour
– but it cannot prevent the genuine amateur from rubbing his
shoulders against many a false amateur whose motives in running
as an amateur are obvious, though no complaint can be made
of his public behaviour.'

This is spoken like a good lawyer, which Shearman was. His
practical solution was to encourage the organisation of professional
athletics and keep it distinct from amateur competition. This did
in fact happen, and a *modus vivendi* was established in the first
decade of the 19th Century. It has never been possible to seal
all the leaks, but after about 1904, when Shrubb lost his amateur
status, athletics in England under the AAA became as amateur
as it was humanly possible for them to be. In 1932, exactly the
abuse which Shearman had mentioned in 1898 – Secretaries of
clubs engaging so-called amateurs at a fixed sum to perform at
their meetings – caused a scandal in Europe, when it was found
that the French runner, Ladoumègue, was receiving something of
the order of £60 a time to appear as the guest-star in various
local French sports meetings. This could certainly not have happened in England at the time, where the AAA enforced its rules
perhaps too rigidly.

Shearman was a great personality with a powerful physique.
He was a fine all-rounder. He ran for Oxford in the 100 yards
and 440 yards, and won the 100 yards at the Amateur Athletic
Club championships, and the 440 yards at the first AAA
Championships. He also played Rugby Football for Oxford, was a

good boxer, rowed in his College boat, and swam Niagara Falls. He was a very successful Barrister, and appointed a Judge of the High Court in 1914, and a Privy Counsellor in 1929. He was the first Honorary Secretary of the AAA, and President from 1916 until his death in January 1930, when his full title of address was the Right Honourable Sir Montague Shearman.

He was a man of outstanding ability, physical and mental, and of great urbanity. His most important contribution to the organisation of athletics, apart from helping to found the AAA, was in reconciling the various conflicting interests. Although his background was Oxford and the 'gentleman amateur', and he believed very strongly in the ideal of the Victorian gentleman, he saw clearly that a nation-wide Athletic Association must be genuinely democratic, and, as Secretary and later President, he saw to it that the non-University and provincial clubs had a full say in any decisions that were made. All this is now taken for granted, but it was not in the very different social climate of 1880. Sir Montague Shearman was one of those who did most to shape athletic competition as it is today, not just in Britain, but all over the world.

The Americans were the first to organise athletics on the British pattern. They repeated the British experience in that there was a conflict between two rival bodies, the National Association of Amateur Athletes of America, which was confined to New York, and the New York Athletic Club which wanted to spread the interest in athletics more widely. The first USA Championships, organised by the New York Athletic Club, were held in 1874. These corresponded to the British Amateur Athletic Club championships held from 1866 to 1879, and were not representative. The equivalent of the AAA was the Amateur Athletic Union, which was founded under pressure from the New York Athletic Club, and held its first really representative national competition in 1888 at Detroit.

As in Britain, the Universities and Colleges were prominent in developing athletics. The first organised international contest in the history of athletics was the match between Yale and Oxford in 1894. There had been a good deal of individual competition between athletes on both sides of the Atlantic, including races both in England and the United States between L. E. Myers and W. G. George.

The Yale-Oxford match was held in July 1894. An American

enthusiast, Charles H. Sherrill, who was responsible for the organisation on the American side of both this match and the Yale-Cambridge match held in New York the following year, wrote a few years later: 'The Yale-Oxford match was the first international track athletic match, as well as the first International Inter-University match in athletic history.' In 1895 the London Athletic Club took over a team to compete with the New York Athletic Club. Thus the foundations of systematic athletic competition had been laid before the first modern Olympiad in 1896, although Baron Coubertin was canvassing his idea as early as January 1894.

The great value of these first Anglo-American exchanges was in showing differences in method and interpretation and so beginning the process of standardisation of rules and events. For instance, the British athletes used fixed hurdles on grass, whereas the Americans used flexible hurdles on the cinder-track, and the Americans used what is now the standard method of shot-putting, in which the elbow had to be behind the shot. The British allowed what the Americans called 'drawing the shot', in which the elbow could lead at the beginning of the throw. They banned this on the ground that an advantage was gained, especially by a big man, from the slight swing in the initial velocity.

The British clubs also found a wholly different approach to athletics. Then, as now, the Americans did nothing by halves, and they duly got results. At the New York AC v. London AC match, they won all eleven events – although some were very closely contested, and the LAC lacked several of their star performers, including C. B. Fry, then still the long-jump record-holder, F. E. Bacon, currently the fastest three- or four-miler, and possibly capable of beating the American champion, Conneff over a mile, and E. C. Bredin, the fastest quarter-miler and half-miler at the time.

Nevertheless, the London Club were soundly beaten, and it was obvious from what they learned then about American methods that only athletes of exceptionally high talent had a chance of beating the highly trained Americans. Charles H. Sherrill wrote: 'We have been accused of making our athletics too much of a business; of having systematised them with more precision and care of details than seems consistent when one considers that, after all, they are only pastimes. To this accusation we must to a certain extent plead guilty, saying nothing more in extenuation than that we are Americans, and that we are simply carrying out our national spirit when we apply to our athletics the newest ideas in the same fashion as we apply them to our businesses and our professions. Our application of system to the development of athletics is particularly noticeable in our larger Universities, where those ambitious for track athletic honours are coached by professional trainers hired for that purpose.' The Americans had thus by the early nineties set the pattern of modern competition.

Sherrill, who was Captain of Athletics at Yale in 1899, also contrasted the management of American University team athletics with the casual approach of the Oxford or Cambridge organisers:

'At Yale and at the other American universities the procedure is quite different. Varsity sports are held in the autumn, but they seldom have any other result than to enable the cracks of the year before who are still in residence to pick up a few prizes, or some freshman with an indecently long handicap to indulge in a bit of mug-hunting. The real work begins when the university comes together after the Christmas vacation. Then the captain issues a call requesting all who wish to try for that year's team to report to the gymnasium. The result is that about one hundred and fifty individuals, all sorts and conditions of men, put in an appearance, each with a more or less fixed idea of which particular branch of track athletics he was ordained by nature to adorn. These applications are divided up into groups, each group being put in the charge of a Blue, whose duty it is to see that his pupils do not start their athletic careers by acquiring bad habits which it would take days of practice to eradicate later in the season.

'The sprinters begin at once at practising starting from the pistol in a long building with a dirt floor, which enables them to use spiked shoes. The middle and long distance men are sent out for long runs in the country. The jumpers practise starting with the sprinters to a limited extent, in order to give them snap and quickness. The pole-vaulters practise their art in the big gymnasium, where the shot-putters are also training. All of these men take a certain amount of light gymnasium work, and all report to the gymnasium each afternoon. All of our larger universities and colleges are provided with ample gymnasium accommodation, and some of them are almost luxurious in their equipment. The gymnasium at Yale was built by the graduates, subscriptions for the fund coming from every part of the country. Besides the usual features of a gymnasium, it has two large rowing tanks, in the centre of each of which is moored a barge. These are used to give practice to the crews in watermanship during the early winter months when the harbour is made dangerous by floating ice. The Hamenway gymnasium at Harvard is also a very spacious building, and is supplemented by the Carey building, containing rowing tanks, etc. The work done in the gymnasiums during the winter is a very valuable part of the training of the track athletic team.

'The captain must not content himself with the fact that he has this large number of candidates as material for his team. He must look about over the university for big men whose strength is combined with quickness, in order that he may get more material with which to strengthen his team with shot-putters and hammer-throwers, as these two require long practice, and January to June is short enough. He must also look out for recruits and inquire into the history of the members of the freshman class, for there may be some men who have shown ability in some form at school and who may be lurking behind a mistaken sense of modesty. These men must be followed up and gotten out to practice. The captain is continually having reported to him by the Blues in charge of the various squads that one promising man has failed to appear at the gymnasium for two or three days, or that another promising man is too ambitious and is overworking himself, and it is the captain's duty to see that all these matters are set right.

'After a couple of months of this sort of training, during which all these men are under the eyes of the professional trainers, and all of them are learning the beginnings of sprinting, hurdling, weight-throwing, pole-vaulting, etc., in the proper and scientific way, and are not developing themselves by haphazard or by chance, it becomes time for the winter games. These are held in a large armoury building, so large that it is possible to have a fifty yards run straight away. Now comes the time for the first separating of the chaff from the wheat. The team is cut down. The men's work becomes more and more specialised. The jumpers confine themselves strictly to jumping and the hurdlers to hurdling. In a few weeks the weather permits the training to be begun on the running ground at the Yale Field, and the season of competition opens. By this time the captain has his team well in hand.

He has them cut down to about fifty or sixty men, and the competition for places on the team grows more sharp. About the middle of May the annual match with Harvard is held.'

Two weeks after this meeting came the Intercollegiate meeting, to which representatives were sent from the various universities and colleges all over the country, at which a cup was awarded to the college winning most points. Sherrill commented – not surprisingly: 'The result of this American system of developing athletes is sometimes astounding.'

The Americans began to stress the element of team competition as soon as College athletics came to be organised, and this provided a popular spectacle which helped to finance athletics, and to pay for facilities incomparably better than athletes have ever enjoyed in Britain. It was in Sherrill's time that they invented the relay race, beginning with 4 x 440 yards.

Incidentally, the first relay race in England was held in 1895 by the Ranelagh Harriers at Stamford Bridge, but the practice did not attract much attention until 1909, when a relay race was included in the Essex County Sports. The event was first included in the AAA Championship in 1911.

All this American enthusiasm and willingness to spend money on the best facilities explains the continuing all-round excellence of United States athletes in international competition, which has only ever been matched by another country of vast resources and intense organising power, the Soviet Union.

3

Amateurs and Professionals

The concept of amateurism, as it now exists in the thinking of the AAA and the Olympic Committee – and scarcely anywhere else – derives from the mentality of the Victorian English gentleman. It was not an accident that the founders of the modern Olympic Games in 1896 adopted by and large the English definition of an amateur. This was a time when the image of the English gentleman was held in high esteem throughout Europe, which was then the civilised world.

The Baron de Coubertin, who did most to promote the idea, came from a French aristocratic family which took a dim view of the Third Republic, formed after the defeat of France by Prussia, and described by the great French historian, Octave Aubry, as '*la liquidation d'un désastre*'. The Baron was concerned with maintaining aristocratic standards in an increasingly egalitarian world. It was natural that he should regard the English gentlemanly ideal as a solid bulwark of decent behaviour, when France was republican, Germany was increasingly turning to nationalist militarism, Russia was bedevilled by a three-sided struggle between liberals, reactionaries and anarchists, and, as Karl Marx had written in 1848, a spectre was stalking Europe, the spectre of Communism.

The English concept of amateurism – and it was English rather than British, because it grew mainly in the Public Schools and Universities of Southern England – was a very Victorian phenomenon.

We have seen how 'pedestrianism' developed in England as a form of professional competition against a background of betting, until at the beginning of the Victorian era it was taken up and practised as a sport of gentlemen. The Victorian puritanical attitudes were a reaction against the licence of a previous era, in the later 18th and early 19th Century, when the morals of the Royal family became an endemic scandal, political corruption was the rule, and the working-classes were degraded by poverty and drunkenness. The Church was as corrupt as politics, and education in schools and Universities was at its lowest ebb.

The revival in education, in the period just about when Victoria became Queen, the great reforming spirit in social and religious life, and the high moral example set by the Monarchy, were all part of the reaction against this corrupt society of the later 18th Century and the Regency, when a gentleman was apt to dissipate his estate and run into debt through profligate living, and especially gambling. The pursuit of more manly sports, like running, football, rowing and cricket, was an aspect of the reforming zeal of headmasters, social reformers, evangelical Christians and others, which went to create the solid Victorian values of honest dealing, independence, self-control, thrift and philanthropy, which were essentially upper middle class virtues. They abound in the novels of Dickens, side by side with examples of the vices they managed on the whole to supplant.

There was also a correlation between horses, railways and amateur running. Throughout the Middle Ages and right up to the new industrial age, the horse had been indispensable, as the sole engine of transport, and it was in the category of what we now call durable consumer goods. It was natural that most of the outdoor sport of people who could afford well-bred horses should centre in equitation. When the railways appeared, they were not only the symbol of the new technological and increasingly bourgeois society. They also took over the main function of the horse, which was gradually relegated to the position of an old family retainer who has lost his function and lives on benevolence.

The process was complete when the motor-car arrived, and the horse lost even its subsidiary function of running 'feeder' services, that is, taking the family to the nearest station or the shops. Naturally the horse, with his endearing traits of character, keeps a warm place in the human heart, and the long-established equine sports continued – there has even been a renaissance of riding since the last world war. But the horse was no longer the inevitable medium of sport and, with increasing urbanisation, organised sports tended to be conducted on foot in playing fields constructed for the purpose. This gave an added impetus to the Victorian ideal of strenuous effort and Spartan pleasures, which are well expressed in Hilaire Belloc's lines:

> 'Swam together in winter rivers,
> Wrestled together under the sun.'

When this cult of strenuous physical exercise, including athletics, was established about the middle of the century, there were two cogent reasons for a distinction to be drawn between amateur and professional. One was the sense of class consciousness which (although it had begun to be eroded with the Industrial Revolution) was still a basic attitude. Gentlemen were 'different' and it did not even occur to them to rub shoulders with the toiling masses, however philanthropic they may have felt towards them. The second reason applied most strongly to athletic competition: corruption through betting.

In other sports, professionalism was integrated. Professional and amateur clubs were distinct, but not apart. They competed against each other, notably in the FA Cup, and before the end of the century some distinguished amateur footballers played for professional clubs without danger to their status. In cricket there were always professionals in the County Clubs, and though they may have used different changing-rooms or come on to the field through a different gate, there was no question of an amateur losing status through competing with professionals. When international cricket started, teams were chosen on merit from amateurs and professionals. The first international cricket match was played in Australia. The English touring team consisted entirely of professionals, but thereafter English teams were a balance of amateurs and professionals, with slightly more professionals until after 1919, when they began to preponderate.

In rowing and Rugby Football the distinction between amateur and professional has lingered: both were minority sports, associated with the Public Schools and Universities. Amateur rowing laws for a long time banned manual workers on the ground that they were gaining undue advantage by developing muscular power in the course of their paid employment. The Rugby distinction, which still applies, was based more on class consciousness, but was perpetuated when professional Rugby grew up with a slightly different code of rules.

The rowing code, barring anyone who was 'by trade or employment a mechanic, artisan or labourer' was at first applied to athletics, but this clause was dropped when the Amateur Athletic Association was founded. The definition of an amateur did, however, still exclude competition between amateurs and professionals. It read: [an amateur is]

'Any person who has never competed in any open competition, or for public money, or for admission money, or with professionals for a prize, public money or admission money, and who has never taught or assisted in the pursuit of athletic exercises as a means of livelihood.'

This was an empirical definition which the founders of the AAA hoped would keep the worst features of professionalism in check. When pedestrian contests were a sport sponsored by gentlemen, the running footman put up by his master in the hope of winning a substantial wager (£1,000 was by no means unusual on a single race) he was, so to speak, under starter's orders. He received a (to him) handsome cut from the £1,000, and acquired grace and favour with his employer. Whatever side-bets spectators might place did not influence him. If he had a flutter himself – even including a 'hedge' on his opponent – it was still in the hope of winning the race himself. To enter into a conspiracy with a third party to defraud his master by letting his opponent win would have been unthinkable, and more than his job was worth.

When, however, the promoter appeared on the scene, and matches were arranged between professionals who were not representing employers, but appearing on their own account for a share of the gate-money, corruption was bound to creep in. Enterprising bookmakers operated in the way that Damon Runyan has immortalised in a later and more varied setting. Runners were 'nobbled' and races 'sold', so that professional pedestrians by 1880 had come to be looked on as one of the lower forms of life. The intelligent and percipient people who founded the AAA had to outlaw these activities from amateur athletics. Hence the clause that an amateur forfeited his status if he stepped on to the same track as a professional.* Of course, there were decent professionals who simply wanted to run their best and, because they had no

* Although this is not explicit in the definition quoted in paragraph 2 above.

private means, support themselves while they were doing it. But in a consciously moral society like the Victorians, it was natural to bar all contact with pitch, which, as everyone knew, since they still read the Scriptures, defiled.

This corruption of professional runners was the most sordid aspect. There was another, less reprehensible, but also dangerous one: pot-hunting. Substantial prizes were given to the winners of events in local sports-meetings, usually in the form of silverware, which could easily be sold for a good proportion of its purchase-price. If a runner gave up his job and went round to meetings weekly in the summer, won a fair proportion of prizes, and sold them, he could make a good living out of his running.

The AAA tried to discourage this in 1880 by making a rule that no prize should be awarded of more than £12 sterling in value, unless it was in the form of a cup or trophy, which must be engraved, so that it was identified, like a clipped railway ticket or a piece of plate lifted from a well-known hotel. This was an unrealistic law. £12 was a lot of money in 1880 when a skilled worker was doing very well on £3 a week. If an unskilled worker took up full time athletics, and was a really good runner, he might easily win twenty prizes of up to £12 value in a season. Even allowing a substantial percentage in selling these prizes, he would still be better off than a skilled worker, quite apart from the 'expenses' he would be paid, as a drawer of crowds, to compete.

Ten years after this AAA rule was passed, there were still professionals to be found (or not detected) entering for races under assumed names and winning substantial prizes, which they sold.

Even when this practice was eradicated, pot-hunting continued. I can recall running in local meetings round about 1930 in which I sometimes won prizes worth more than a week's salary as a teacher or lecturer. I then felt strongly about amateur status, and always gave my prizes away, but I could have substantially increased my income by a judicious application of my athletic talent.

The AAA rules of 1880 were probably the best that could be devised at the time to deal with the immediate problem. £12 was much too high, but if it had been set at, say, £5, it would still not have done the trick. Amateurism is an attitude of mind. It is easy to propagate among disinterested people with no serious economic problems, as against people who are not sure where their next pound or dollar is coming from. But there were many other stresses which neither the AAA nor Baron Coubertin and his friends could appreciate in the 19th Century.

The tradition of handicap races at local sports-meetings was simply a projection of the old village sports, where appropriate prizes were given – even to the athlete who could win a live pig by carrying it in a race or catching it. The abuse by pot-hunters did not strike at the heart of the amateur definition. Far more important was the *kudos*, regional and national, won by the outstanding athlete, ('The time you won your town the race') and this presented an insoluble problem when international competition developed and introduced the element of national prestige.

The Greeks had been through it all before, when cities offered their citizenship (and a high signing-on fee) to Olympic athletes. This ruined amateur sport, but at first assisted national cohesion, since the Games were Greek and brought all the scattered and dissident Greeks together in pursuit of a Hellenist ideal. The founders of the modern Olympics had this very much in mind. They were romantic admirers of Hellenic ideals as an antidote to industrialism and proletarian manners, but they had read the lesson of the dangers of professionalism from their Hellenic studies. What they did not foresee was the development of a centrifugal nationalism which was to split Europe, and the rest of the world, instead of promoting common ideals and culture.

International competition began tentatively in the nineties.* It was not firmly established by the early Olympic contests at Athens and Paris, or even St Louis, which was remote from the European centres of civilisation. The turning-point was the London Olympiad of 1908, held in the greatest city of the world, at the centre of the greatest Empire the world had seen. This IV Olympiad was the biggest, best organised and most genuinely international to date. There were about 450 entries from twenty countries, and although the United States and Britain won the bulk of the prizes, there was a reasonably wide spread of success. A South African won the 100 metres, a Canadian the 200 metres; an Italian was second in the 800 metres, with a German third and a Hungarian fourth.

* There was a match between England and Ireland in 1876, but Ireland was not then independent.

Dorando Pietri of Italy stole the show in the Marathon. In the javelin Swedes were first and third, a Norwegian second and Finns took the next three places. Finland and Hungary figured in the first six in the discus. In fact, there were non-Anglo-Saxon names scattered right through the list. The 1904 Games at St Louis had been virtually an American monopoly, but from 1908 onwards all Europe was in with a chance. This was more pronounced in 1912, and in 1913 the International Amateur Athletics Federation was founded. Athletics had become a branch of international relations.

It had been established early on – by the 1880 inaugural meeting of the AAA, accepting decisions already made in the North and Midlands – that competition was open to all classes. Once competition became a question of national prestige, the amateur definition was a dead letter. No nation which believes its prestige is enhanced by athletic success will allow its athletes to be handicapped by their financial circumstances. The one exception was Britain, where the old gentleman-amateur concept died very hard, and still will not lie down. Elsewhere, steps were taken to assist athletes with potential.

In the United States, the problem scarcely arose. There is so much private money to siphon off from the vast wealth of American industry, and so much enthusiasm, that almost anything can be subsidised without State control, from top-class athletic facilities at College or University, to emigré organisations for the subversion of Communist Governments. The traditional idea of athletics scholarships is a gross over-simplification. There are certainly instances of young men being given a scholarship primarily to achieve athletic excellence, but most American student-athletes have been genuine students as well as athletes. They were merely following the pattern of the older British Universities which provided good facilities for training within a framework of not too exacting academic studies. That there are far more, and better-equipped, Colleges and Universities in the United States, per head of population, than in Britain is an American virtue. American Universities and clubs have also been far better equipped to promote athletic excellence, ever since the eighties of the last century, than their British (or even Continental) counterparts.

Nevertheless, the aid which American athletes received to develop their potential was certainly not in accordance with what was meant by the AAA and the Olympic definitions of amateurism.

Other countries allowed their athletes to be assisted in one way or another. The great succession of French athletes, from Jean Bouin onwards, received their main support from private or at most municipal sources. It was only after General de Gaulle came back as President to reinforce the authority of the central Government and restore 'la gloire' to France, that French athletes obtained systematic help and subvention from the Government. In this sense, France gained Great Power status by being the third country to set up a training camp with full facilities at an altitude of 7,000 ft after the decision was made to hold the 1968 Olympic Games in Mexico City.

There was an outstanding precedent for State subvention of athletics for reasons of national prestige. Before the 1936 Berlin Games, which were organised on a more grandoise scale than any before them, a Government directive was sent round to all German Civil Service departments saying that leave with full pay must be granted for a period of up to three months before the beginning of the Olympiad to all Olympic candidates, that is, all athletes who were regarded as possible selections for the German Olympic contingent. This directive applied to all public or municipal employees, from Permanent Under-Secretaries to dustmen, including all school and University teachers and students. The candidates were to be allowed to attend, free of charge and with full pay, a number of resident training camps which had been set up with all facilities, including coaching and medical attention,* to get them up to peak performance for the Games.

A copy of this directive was conveyed to the Committee of the AAA, with the suggestion that it violated the rules of amateur competition, and most flagrantly the 'broken time' rule which had been the subject of much controversy. This rule forbade payment equivalent to the earnings lost by an athlete during the time taken off to compete. Many people regarded it as inequitable. An athlete with private means lost nothing. One in salaried employment who could get permission to take a day or some days off for competition received his usual cheque at the end of the month. But a working-class athlete, paid by the shift or the hour, for-

---

* In this period German Universities had set up special faculties of 'Sport Medicine'.

Above: Wooderson: the stride that Zatopek did not believe (p.73). *Below:*
Paavo Nurmi and the Author, London 1930

Above: Last lap at Helsinki: Zatopek, Schade, Reiff and Chataway. Pirie is seventh. *Below:* The end of the road for Jim Peters: Vancouver 1954

feited his earnings, and was probably the least able to afford this. Nevertheless, the rule was still regarded as sacrosanct by officials (mostly independent or salaried).

The Nazi directive was a straightforward violation of the 'broken-time' rule, and it was argued that it made all German competitors who benefited automatically professionals. It followed that any British athlete who took part in the Berlin Games would be competing with professionals and therefore just as liable as W. G. George in 1885 to forfeit his amateur status. Therefore the AAA ought to decline to send a team to the Games.

This was not the AAA's finest hour. The Committee decided (it is understood by a close vote) not to pursue the matter. There was plenty of legalistic sand for ostriches. It could be argued that the German equivalent of the AAA (by then the German National Socialist Amateur Athletic Association) manned by Nazis, would not easily be persuaded to declare all their best athletes professionals, whatever Olympic rules might say: Hitler never showed any great sensitivity about international conventions. As long as the Germans were not actually professional at the time of competition, British athletes would not be affected.

Whatever the arguments, this was one of the sad steps on the road to appeasement, but the AAA should not be unduly reproached. It is difficult to believe that other national associations did not know about this Nazi directive. An initiative from the AAA would probably have had the effect of causing a boycott of the Berlin Olympics by many nations. They would probably have become a sort of Axis Games between Germany, Italy, Japan and Hungary. Viewing the matter with hindsight, we may think this would have been a good thing, but the climate of opinion in Britain and elsewhere was far from steady for the confrontation: most people preferred to believe it would never happen. And, after all, the AAA is not the Foreign Office. Its job is to organise athletics fairly in Britain and promote international exchanges, and boycotts in one field do not solve problems in others.

Where the AAA is vulnerable is in still to this day adhering blindly to an amateur definition which has never been realistic since the Nazi directive in 1936 blew it up sky-high.

After the war, when a large number of countries which are fully state-controlled joined in international competition, the amateur definition became more and more irrelevant. Nationalist sentiment

D

had crept into the Olympic competitions very early on, but since the last war nationalism has become the great, burning emotion governing international relations (and threatening us all with extinction). To expect that amateur rules proper to English Victorian gentlemen a century ago can be relevant in this day and age is myopic in the extreme.

No one without a private income or some form of subvention can possibly carry out the exhausting training schedules now required for success in top-class competition, unless he is in one of the professions which allow him to combine a big volume of training with his work: a soldier, Physical Education teacher or student for instance. But there is no particular reason why people in these limited categories should be classed as amateurs, while those who cannot combine their training schedules with their work should either give up competition or be barred as professionals.

In practice, most of them find a way. In the Soviet Union, the State is the employer and can call the tune. When Soviet talent-spotters find a prospective champion who can boost the prestige of the Soviet Union in international competition, the State wills the means as well as the end. The athlete is not directly paid to compete, but he is given a nominal job which frees him from financial worry, together with all facilities for training and improvement. This may not be the ideal system for bringing out the best in a long-distance runner of genius, but it guarantees a very high average standard from which a whole succession of distinguished international performers can be drawn.

Other countries have other methods, and they all keep more or less within the letter of the law of amateurism, but very few athletes in this day and age comply with the spirit, and it is difficult to think of any practical reason why they should, because the letter and the spirit of the law belong to a defunct society. The Olympic idea is constantly threatened by extraneous influences, nationalist, ideological, racial and commercial. So far, it has survived them, and probably will for some time to come, because the Olympic idea, whatever its faults or confusions, has a great dynamic. The one weakness it cannot afford is cynicism. The danger is in pretending that rules are being observed when everyone knows they are not.

When Mr Avery Brundage, the I.O.C President, went to the

Soviet Union in 1952 to investigate allegations that Soviet athletics violated the amateur definition, he said that he could find no evidence that it did. This was a gross error. He should have said: 'Of course it does, and so does athletics in the United States, France, Germany, Finland, Australia and Japan (to mention only six). It follows from this that there is something wrong with the definition. Let us therefore get round a table and find an agreed formula for dragging the definition screaming into the second-half of the Twentieth Century.'

Few Olympic athletes (at any rate of the high IQ type who succeed at long distances) have any illusions about the amateur definition. Emil Zatopek, who has successfully combined soldiering with athletics without ever breaking (or even bending) the rules, believes that they are irrelevant. He points out that athletes in under-developed countries are at a great disadvantage. There it is not a question of an athlete making money out of athletics, but of his getting access to the minimum of facilities (including diet) which will put him on anything like equal terms with an athlete from a developed country. Zatopek argues for equality of opportunity for all athletes. As this is precisely what the existing rules legislate against, they should be scrapped.

Ron Clarke also does not think the rules make sense. He cannot see why top-class public performers should dip into their own pockets to subsidise promoters and spectators, any more than an actor should work for nothing. He thinks the present rules should be scrapped, as in tennis or cricket.

Christopher Chataway was an amateur of the Oxford school, who combined running with the building up of a career. He suggests that the amateur definition is well out of date and that there should be two classes of athletes: those concerned about amateur status, who would mainly operate at a lower level of performance and enjoy their running without trying to go through the immense effort needed for top-level performance, and those who are prepared to make that effort, regardless of status. This resembles what has already happened in Association Football. After a farcical period in which genuine amateurs competed in Olympic Soccer against players who were by their standards high-class professionals, it was wisely decreed that no footballer could be eligible both for the World Cup and for the Olympic Soccer competition. This has removed much of the interest from Olympic

Soccer, but it has clarified the amateur definition, although some countries draft in players who were World Cup reserves.

In athletics it would be disastrous if the 'pure' amateurs took over the Olympic Games, and the top-class competition was held elsewhere. It would mean the end of the Olympic Games as we have seen them for the past 72 years. Amateur soccer and boxing, basket-ball and ice-hockey (which are both very suspect from a purist amateur view), horse-jumping, swimming and various *miscellanea* would not of themselves create a world sporting event. It all hangs on the athletics. If these became second-grade, like the Football and the minority sports, the Olympic Games would die, and this would be a great pity. The practical solution is to abolish the 19th Century amateur formula and throw the Games open to the best competitors, with certain carefully thought-out rules to prevent abuses.

These rules would be aimed at preventing the corruption of athletes by gambling or other forms of commercialism, and could be safely left to the international athletic associations to enforce.

The decision to hold the next Olympics in Mexico City has raised this question of the amateur definition in a big way. It has been fairly well established that performers in 'explosive' events – jumping, throwing and running at distances up to 400 metres, and perhaps even 800 metres – will not suffer, but the 'endurance' events will be affected by the shortage of oxygen in the air at that altitude, as against sea-level. The Olympic Committee has issued a pious directive that athletes must not train for more than four weeks at the operative level before the Games.*
This is typical of the attitude of the Olympic Committee towards amateurism. Half a dozen countries have facilities for training their athletes at the Mexico City altitude. The French *Union des Sports Athlétiques* has generously offered its facilities for high-altitude training to athletes of other countries and no doubt the other nations with similar facilities, the United States, the Soviet Union, the German Federal Republic, Ethiopia and Kenya would be prepared to do the same.

The point is, however, that very few amateurs – that is, people who do not earn any part of their living from athletics – can possibly spend a minimum of four weeks, in addition to the three or

* i.e. in Mexico City immediately before the Games.

four weeks they must write off for the Games themselves, in special training in a remote place. Nor can the Olympic Committee establish whether any competitor at Mexico City has in fact trained for not more than 4 weeks above 7,000 feet. Ethiopians and Kenyans do almost all their training at that altitude, anyway, and it would be absurd to exclude them because they had continued their normal training.

It was perhaps an error of judgment to decide to hold the Games in Mexico City, but most athletes accept it as an Olympic risk. It will mean that Ron Clarke will be at a disadvantage against his chief rival, Keino,* and any American, French or Soviet runners in his class. He accepts this without rancour, although it could mean that he, as the indisputably best runner at his distance over a period of 4 years, may never win an Olympic gold medal. If the Australian Government, or some wealthy sponsor, could build him a pressure-chamber to train in, and if he could take off enough time from his work to go through the special training schedule, he would have an equal chance with everyone else. The probability is that he will not.

In any case, it would sooner or later have been discovered that training at high altitudes gives an overall advantage, and this fact is more important than a single Olympiad. It is only fair that all athletes should have an opportunity of doing it for periods in every season, and this cannot possibly be provided without bending the amateur definition out of all recognisable shape. It would be necessary for National associations to provide the finance to give athletes facilities at high-level camps in their own or neighbouring countries.

This new factor of altitude running and training should thus finally have disposed of the Victorian concept of gentlemen-amateurs. In the future there should be no unenforceable regulations which handicap those who observe them and favour those who do not. Top-class competition in athletics should be thrown open to top-class performers. The rules should simply aim at preventing corruption. They should bar anyone who is obviously exploiting athletics for commercial ends. They should not bar a man who is given a nominal job, by his Government or by a private firm, which provides him with bed and board and facilities for training. They could not – any more than the existing rules – prevent him from becoming a newspaper or television personality when he gives up athletics, but they could easily stop him from earning lavish fringe-benefits while he is actually competing. Any competent lawyer could draft regulations to cover these points, just as a lawyer and two law students drafted the original AAA rules to cover the difficulties in 1880.

It is sad that the AAA, which once led the world in the organisation of athletics, should be on present showing the last authority to bring itself up to date. When the present (or past) generation of AAA officials gives way to athletes who have competed since 1946, the Association may again be in a position to give a lead, as it so creditably did 88 years ago. Lawn Tennis was also a game for gentlemen (and ladies) but the All-England Lawn Tennis Club has given a realistic and courageous lead to the rest of the world in abolishing 'shamateurism'. The AAA, with its great tradition, could do the same for athletics.

4

The Proto-Champions

As we have seen, organised long-distance competition came back in mid-19th Century England, when the popular sports – professional pedestrianism for stakes, and cross-country running in rural England – were focussed by patrician schools and University Colleges into a worthwhile exercise for gentlemen. This may have been class-conscious but it created modern athletics. The element of professionalism by no means disappeared – or its terminology: Alfred Shrubb as late as 1910 consistently refers to distance running as pedestrianism, and the term survived World War I. After the AAA had succeeded in introducing in 1880 a nation-wide organisation for amateur competition, with standard practices and rules, professional contests continued in what might be called the private sector. Some professionals went on as before and would have nothing to do with the amateur associations; other likely lads chose to use their talents commercially; and, as the century went on, some distinguished amateurs found themselves shunted into the professional sector, willy-nilly.

In the earlier years of this epoch, professional standards were generally higher than amateur in the distance events. After the 1860s, when statistical consciousness grew, both amateur and professional records were kept. Thanks to the AAC and AAA, amateur records were at first more reliable, but by the eighties of the century time-keeping had become generally efficient. By then, amateur performances outstripped professional, with one qualification, because the best athletes were attracted to the higher status of national and international competition afforded by the AAA. The qualification was the case of leading amateurs who turned professional for one reason or another. Walter Goodall George, born at Calne, Wilts, in 1858, the first great modern distance runner, having won everything there was to be won under amateur conditions, chose professionalism not for profit but to find other worlds to conquer.

George had run a mile in 4.26$\frac{1}{5}$ in 1879, and achieved 4.18$\frac{2}{5}$ in 1884, an amateur world record which stood till 1893, when the Irish-born American Thomas Conneff returned 4.17$\frac{4}{5}$ at Cambridge, Mass. Two years later Conneff improved on this in New York with 4.15$\frac{3}{5}$, a record that stood till 1911. But in the meanwhile, in 1884, George heard that a Scottish professional, William Cummings, had run a mile in 4.16$\frac{1}{5}$ – 2 seconds inside his own amateur record – and wanted to compete against him. As this was barred by AAA rules, he gave up his amateur status and in August 1885 beat Cummings in London in a time of 4.12$\frac{3}{4}$, which remained the fastest on record, apart from a performance by the American Norman Taber in 1913, which was not done under normal conditions, until Nurmi beat it in 1923.

George's performance could not stand as an amateur record, but there is no doubt about its authenticity. It was run before a large crowd at the Lillie Bridge ground in London, and the time-keeping was sufficiently sophisticated to record the lap-times. Moreover, George was a professional only on a technical point, of competing against a professional: his training and facilities had not otherwise changed. He was emphatically a competitive runner who pulled out his best against top-class opposition, which was the one advantage he got from his professional status.

George was also a fast half-miler by current standards. In 1882 he won the AAA half-mile in 1.58$\frac{2}{5}$. His greatest year was 1884 when he took the AAA half-mile, mile, 4 miles and 10 miles championships, at a two-day meeting. Altogether he won 12 championship medals between 1879 and 1884. His 4 miles world record of 20.17$\frac{4}{5}$ stood for 10 years, and his 10 miles 51.10, for 20 years (it remained English native record for 50 years). He was also twice National Cross-Country champion.

George did not train intensively by modern standards. He got his peak fitness by racing weekly in 2 or 3 events. There were other runners who drove him and sometimes even beat him at one distance or another, but what makes him the first of the really great runners, the 'proto-champions', is his combination of pace and endurance, which made him almost unbeatable from one mile upwards.

Finnish runners. By 1920 he was in world class. He went Antwerp Olympics with Hannes Kohlemainen and was d against the French runner, Joseph Guillemot, over 5,000 0,000 metres. Guillemot won a good tactical victory in the metres, but Nurmi won the 10,000 metres by about 10

the following years, Nurmi systematised his training further, ially by checking lap-times to ensure even-paced running. He to carry a stop-watch on his wrist and glance at it every round. During the next 10 years he broke 20 world records listances from 1,500 metres up to the 1 hour. He did not, some modern runners, start at the shorter distances and work His first world record was 10,000 metres (30.40.2) in 1921. n 1923 he ran a mile in $4.10\frac{3}{5}$, knocking more than 2 seconds George's long-standing professional record of $4.12\frac{3}{4}$ and the nateur record of the American Norman Taber, $4.12\frac{3}{5}$, set up in ther dubious circumstances at Cambridge, Massachusetts in 913. The race was a handicap organised for the attempt on the ecord, and one competitor dropped out before the finish in order o allow Taber to win the race, since his record would not otherwise have been valid under the rules at the time. Both George and Nurmi ran under fully competitive conditions. Nurmi also broke the 3 miles record, in the same year. His finest year was 1924, when he set up records over 4 and 5 miles and, in Olympic trials at Helsinki in June, broke the 1,500 metres and 5,000 metres records in races just over 1 hour apart.

At the Olympic Games in Paris the following month he ran 7 races in 6 days (including heats for the 1,500 metres, 5,000 metres and 3,000 metres team race). On 10th July he had 2 races (1,500 metres and 5,000 metres finals) within 75 minutes. He won both in Olympic and world record times. 2 days later, he won the 10,000 metres cross-country race which was described as 'the most catastrophic event in the history of long-distance running'. It was run in a heatwave, and two-thirds of the competitors collapsed and many of them had to be taken to hospital. Nurmi finished remarkably fresh, and on the following day comfortably won the final of the 3,000 metres team race. This was the most versatile performance at an Olympiad until Zatopek in 1952 won the 5,000 metres, 10,000 metres and the Marathon.

Nurmi did not compete in the 10,000 metres at the Paris Games,

The second great distance runner in George's class, and the first in the modern tradition of systematic training, was Alfred Shrubb, born at Slinfold, Sussex, in December 1878. He began running with the local club, Horsham Harriers, and at once went to the top, sweeping the board in club races and in the Sussex County Championships, and then the National Championships at 1 mile, 4 miles and 10 miles. Between 1900 and 1904 he won the AAA mile twice, the 4 miles and 10 miles 4 times each. He also won the National Cross-country Championship 4 times, and when the International Cross-country Championship was started in 1903 he won it for the first 2 years. This last feat meant less than may appear, as the International was a monopoly for the British Isles until the great French distance runner, Jean Bouin, emerged in 1911.

Shrubb had less panache than George. His physique was slight: he stood about 5 ft. 7 in. (1.65 metres) and weighed $8\frac{1}{2}$ stone (119 lb.) when fully trained, but he was well-proportioned, and ran with a fluent, economical action which made his stride appear longer than it was (he tells us that it was just under 5 ft.). He never had, or tried to acquire, real pace, and seldom beat 4.30 for a mile.

His last performance as an amateur was at Ibrox Park in November 1904, when he ran $11\frac{3}{4}$ miles in 60 mins, $32\frac{1}{5}$ secs, setting up new records for 6, 7, 8, 9, 10 and 11 miles and one hour en route. Shrubb was justly proud of all these records, but the only 2 officially accepted were the 6 miles and 10 miles. The latter did not last very long, but the 6 miles record of $29.59\frac{2}{5}$ stood until 1930, when Nurmi broke it. This longevity was partly because 6 miles was a rare distance until 1932. Both Nurmi and Ritola had already achieved a faster equivalent over 10,000 metres.

The race at Ibrox Park had proved to be Shrubb's swan-song as an amateur. His spectacular success and his advertised training schedules led the AAA to investigate his amateur status, which he lost. He continued to run for some years as a professional, but did not better his performances. He indulged in some freak racing, on one occasion against a champion trotting horse which, by a desperate 'kick' in the last lap beat him by 15 yards, on another against a relay team of 5 Americans, whom he beat.

Shrubb was the progenitor of even-paced running. At Ibrox Park he covered his first mile in $4.44\frac{1}{5}$ and averaged about 5 mins

5 secs a mile up to 6 miles. Thereafter, he eased down to about 5 mins 12 secs per mile up to 10 miles and then slowed to about 1 min 24 secs per lap for the last 1¾ miles, that is a rate of 5 mins 36 secs per mile. Taking the nature of the race into account – an attempt on 3 records from 6 miles to 1 hour – this is very even running. If he had been aiming at the 6 miles only, he could well have pulled 10 seconds off his sixth mile, which would have given a schedule similar to Nurmi's when he beat the record in 1930. Nurmi on that occasion covered his first mile in 4.45 and stayed almost exactly on 5 minutes a mile for the next 4, finishing with a sixth mile at 4.50 which gave him a net result of 29.36.

Shrubb's training schedules were based on regular, methodical work. In his book, *Running and Cross Country Running*, he details his programmes for the period 6th October to 4th November 1904, in preparation for his great run at Ibrox Park. (He also records a diary of his weight, which varied from 122 lb. at the start to 119 lb. at the end, and went down to 118 after some of his harder training runs.) He did not train for pace (except that he always finished his work-outs with about 100 yards full out to induce a habit of sprinting to the tape). His lowest distance at speed was 2 miles which he did either 'fast' or timed at racing speed. He ran every day except Sundays and one Friday when he felt off colour, and usually twice a day. Apart from hard 2-mile spells, he ran 'steady' at from 3 to 8 miles, alternating slower with faster work in the morning and afternoon stints. He never ran more than 10 miles at a stretch, but, since his main ambition was to lower George's 20-year-old 10 mile record, he ran 3 10-mile 'trials' at weekly intervals during the second-half of his schedule. In all three he was timed inside George's record.*

Anyone studying the schedule and knowing that Shrubb was not a man of private means can scarcely be surprised at the outcome of the enquiry into his amateur status. It was estimated by an admirer (Mr J. Murray) that in 6 years he collected 'amateur' prizes to a value of £2,000.

After Shrubb, the next proto-champion might have been the Frenchman, Jean Bouin, who was born at Marseilles on 28th December 1888. As we have seen, he broke the British monopoly in the Cross-country International race, which he won in 1911

* See page 65.

and 1912. He was a very hard wo distances and also foreshadowed st gymnastics. In 1911 he broke Shrubb' completing 11 miles 968 yards (18,588

In the Olympic Games of 1912, the races were introduced, and Bouin was e This was odd, because in November 191 record for 10,000 metres, which stood 1924. Hannes Kohlemainen, the first of th was entered for both races. He won the were heats both that year and in 1920). Tw heats of the 5,000, in which Bouin put up a the following day, the final of the 5,000 greatest Olympic race since the beginnin Kohlemainen won it by less than 2 yards afte the way.

In 1913, Bouin improved on his 1 hour rec 1,442 yards (19,015 metres). He was then only 24 the pace and stamina to open up, with Kohlema in distance running, but *dis aliter visum*. He was in Flanders in 1914.

Kohlemainen was not actively involved in the 191 it took away 4 of the best years of his athletic l brothers, Tatu and William, who were both marathon founded the great Finnish school of athletes who distance running between the two wars. With its most product Nurmi, we need no longer speak of proto-c Hannes Kohlemainen rounded his career by winning the marathon race in 1920.

Parvo Nurmi, born at Turku, Finland on 13th June 18 the prototype of the modern athlete. He made running k art and a science and put the seal of his admirable pers on it. He was a legend and a pattern: like Hotspur,

> 'He was the mark and glass, copy and book,
> That fashioned others.'

It is difficult today, after the spate of high quality competiti of the last 20 years to appreciate the immense impact of Nurn on athletics in the twenties. Between 1917 and 1919, under the guidance of the Kohlemainen family, he became the best of the

younge
to the
match
and 1
5,000
yards
In
espe
used
time
at
like
up

of
a
r
1

which was won by Ritola in a time which broke Nurmi's own recent world record.* The following month, back in Finland, Nurmi set up a new 10,000 metres record (30.06⅕) which stood till 1937, when it was reduced by ⅔ of a second. His last record, in 1931, at the age of 34, was the 2 miles, at 8.59.5. He had already been the first to beat 9 minutes for this distance, but that was on an indoor track at Madison Square Garden which, owing to banking and resilience, was rated faster than any outdoor track.

Like Shrubb, Nurmi put in a great deal of work in training. He ran more and longer than Shrubb, but he also did not train for speed. He ran the half-mile or 800 metres several times in about 1.56, that is, a little faster than George ran in 1884. A mile race between George as he was in 1884-5 and Nurmi as he was 40 years later would have been a great event and would certainly have brought the mile record well inside 4 mins 10 secs.

Nurmi's importance was not in mile-running, except in showing that a great distance runner must be able to give the best milers a run for their money. His importance was in systematising running above the mile. In his long career he was beaten a few times, but so rarely that it was never taken seriously. He set up a whole range of records, which stood for a long time. When, in his running life, some of them were broken, it was recognised that records are made to be broken, and it was generally thought that he could re-make them if he wished. It is significant that in his last full season, when younger men were clipping his times, he set up his 2 miles record in Helsinki against his 3 best successors, Lehtinen, Virtanen and Iso-Hollo, and he came from behind to overtake Lehtinen in the last 200 yards and beat him by 8 yards.

He always planned his races to do what was necessary to win or to break a record, and only rarely had to pull all the stops out.

Nurmi's records were gradually, but only marginally, eroded. In 1926, Otto Peltzer beat him, and his 1,500 metres record, in a magnificent race in Berlin in which Edvin Wide was second and only 1.8 seconds separated the 3 runners. In 1931 Jules Ladoumègue of France brought the mile time down to 4.9½ and Lovelock and others reduced this further, as we shall see below. The longer distances were attacked by the Finnish school. In 1937

* Nurmi beat Ritola in the 10,000 metres at the Amsterdam Olympics in 1928, and Ritola won the 5,000 metres.

Ilmari Salminen broke the last of Nurmi's official records, the 10,000 metres, but only by ⅔ of a second. In 1932 Lauri Lehtinen and Volmari Iso-Hollo both beat his 5,000 metres time and Lehtinen's new record was 14.16.9, just over 11 seconds faster than Nurmi's. The 2 miles and 3,000 metres records were also broken by Janusz Kosucinski of Poland and Taisto Måki. But none of these margins were sufficient to suggest that Nurmi himself at any time up till 1932 could not have matched them. Taisto Måki in 1939 reduced the 5,000 metres to 14 mins 8 secs and the 10,000 to 29 mins 52 secs.

Nurmi had hoped to round off his career like Hannes Kohlemainen, by winning the Olympic marathon: the only title from 1,500 metres upwards that he had not held. Unfortunately, he lost his amateur status in 1932 just before the Los Angeles Olympiad. He was the victim of a somewhat sordid feud in the International Amateur Athletic Federation. Jules Ladoumègue had been guilty of a series of infringements of amateur rules and was impeached by the Finnish delegate and suspended. This caused great annoyance to the French authorities, as Ladoumègue had good prospects in the Olympic 1,500 metres, so a counter-charge was made against Nurmi who, like many other prominent athletes of the time, could be shown to have infringed IAAF standards. It was an unfortunate episode and particularly sad in excluding Nurmi from what would have been the climax of his career.

In the period from Nurmi's retirement till the outbreak of war, distance running was dominated by the next generation of Finns, inspired and advised by Nurmi. At the Olympics of 1932 and 1936, they won 5 gold medals, 4 silver and 3 bronze, as well as two 4th places and a 6th. The only 'foreigner' who broke into the preserve was Kosucinsky of Poland, who took the 10,000 metres in 1932. The Finns also won third place in the marathon in 1932 and fourth and fifth places in 1936. The group who achieved this were Lauri Lehtinen, Lauri Virtanen, Volmari Iso-Hollo (who took the steeple-chase both times) and G. Hockert, but none of these had anything like the sustained all-round excellence of Nurmi. Nor did the other top-class distance runners, Kosucinsky of Poland and Ralph Hill of the USA. No British runners in that period came into the top-class except in the marathon.

Taisto Måki, who came to the front after the 1936 Olympics,

was the nearest to Nurmi in range. He won the European 5,000 metres championship in 1938, and in 1939 broke records in the 2 miles (8.53.2), 3 miles (13.42.4), 5,000 metres (14.8.8), 6 miles (28.55.6) and 10,000 metres (29.52.6). He also ran 1,500 metres in 3.53.5 (equivalent to about a 4.5 mile). In his 10,000 metres record run, in which he was the first to break 30 minutes, his pacing was remarkably even: he covered the first half in 14.58.2 and the second in 14.54.4. But for the War, he would most probably have set his mark on the 1940 Olympics, which were to be held in Helsinki.

After 1939, came the Swedish school, in which Gundar Haegg was outstanding. He was fortunate that, owing to Sweden's neutrality, he was able to continue first-class athletics during the war. He was unlucky in that he had no international competition to draw him out; but he was again fortunate in having a group of high quality runners to train and compete with – a new Swedish school which took over from the Finnish. Among these, Arne Andersson was also outstanding.

The Swedish school derived from the Finns, and especially the technique of Paavo Nurmi which again was an extension of Shrubb's methods. Its training was based on the system called *Fartlek* (a 'portmanteau' word which combines the roots of the Swedish words for 'running' and 'pleasure', and is usually translated 'speed-play'). This was devised by the Swedish National Coach, Gosta Olander in collaboration with Henry Kalärne, a fine middle-distance runner who for a time held the world 3,000 metres record.* They set up a camp at Valadälen among the pine-forests of Jamtland, Central Sweden, where athletes could train in natural circumstances, running as far and as fast as they wished, and getting pleasure from their training. There was some Nordic mysticism about the idea, but it worked well in giving runners their basic training under good psychological conditions. It also involved strength training, as they ran in sand-dunes and up hills. When they got on to the track for their intensive, systematic work, they had developed stamina and the taste for running.

Gundar Haegg chipped ½ seconds off Lovelock's 1,500 metres record in 1941, and then, during the summer of 1942, broke all world records from 1,500 metres to 5,000 metres, including a mile

---

* He finished 3rd in the 1936 Olympic 5,000 metres under his original name of Johnson, which he changed.

in 4.04.6. In 1943 he was invited to the United States where he did not improve on any of his records, but gave a great stimulus to American mile running. While Haegg was in America, Arne Andersson ran a mile in 4.02.6. Haegg in 1945 knocked a second off this and the '4 minute' mile was in sight, but our concern here is with the longer distances.

Haegg was a pace-runner who set a new pattern. His first aim was the mile and 1,500 metres, but he had undergone stamina-building training to improve his performance. He moved on naturally to 3,000 metres and 2 miles and thence to 5,000 metres. He improved on Måki's record over 3 miles and was the first runner to bring the 5,000 metres below 14 minutes, when he ran 13.58.2 at Goteberg in 1942. Oddly enough, he did not really like the longer distance because he felt frustrated at having to gear himself down to a pace lower than a miler's. But he set the pattern of a new type, or sub-division, of runner, which might be called 'fast-distance', that is a man who can (by current standards) beat 4 minutes for a mile and run 3 miles at a pace which even 40 years ago would have yielded 3 creditable separate miles. C. J. Chataway is one example.

One other athlete should be mentioned. The last of the dominant Finns, Viljo Heino, was, like so many other runners, unfortunate in losing international competition during the war years which to him were especially important as he was 25 when the war started. He conformed to the Finnish pattern of running best from 2 miles to 10,000 metres. He competed against Haegg in the autumn of 1944 and beat him narrowly over 3,000 metres, 2 miles, and 5,000 metres, in each case improving on the world record. He had already brought the 10,000 metres record down to 29.35.4.

Full international competition was resumed with the 1946 European Games. The Englishman, Sydney Wooderson, who had been the pre-eminent mile runner just before the war and had also lost 5 of his best years of competition, re-emerged in these Games at the age of 32 to win the 5,000 metres from a distinguished field: Slykhuis of Holland, Nyberg of Sweden, Heino, Emil Zatopek and Gaston Reiff of Belgium. Wooderson's time – 14.08.6 – was the second fastest on record.

This race put both Zatopek and Czechoslovakia on the map of athletics.

Landy and Bannister in the 'Mile of the Century': Vancouver 1954

Chataway and Kuts: the 'Race of the Century' – 5,000 metres: London, October 1954

Shrubb's Training Schedule, October-November 1904
(Running and Cross-Country Running, p. 32 ff)

Date	Morning work	Afternoon work	Weight stripped
6th Oct	3 miles fairly slow..	6 miles at decent pace	122 lb
7th Oct	4 miles good pace ..	5 miles good pace ..	120 lb
8th Oct	4 miles good pace ..	Wet, did not go out	120 lb
9th Oct	Sunday		122 lb
10th Oct	3 miles fairly fast ..	3 miles slow..	121 lb
11th Oct	2 miles fast..	6 miles slow..	120½ lb
12th Oct	Did not run	6 miles medium	120 lb
13th Oct	3 miles good pace ..	4 miles medium	119¾ lb
14th Oct	5 miles steady	Did not run ..	120 lb
15th Oct	Brisk walk ..	3 miles fast ..	119½ lb
16th Oct	Sunday		121 lb
17th Oct	8 miles steady	2 miles fast burst ..	120¾ lb
18th Oct	4 miles good pace ..	2 miles (9 mins 18 secs)	120 lb
19th Oct	Did not run	10-mile trial (51 mins 10 secs)	119 lb
20th Oct	5 miles steady	Did not run ..	118½ lb
21st Oct	Did not run	2-mile burst ..	119¼ lb
22nd Oct	6 miles goodish pace	8 miles slow..	118¼ lb
23rd Oct	Sunday		119¾ lb
24th Oct	4 miles steady	2 miles (9 mins 17 4/5 secs)	119 lb
25th Oct	Did not run	10-mile trial (51 mins 2 secs)	118¼ lb
26th Oct	4 miles steady	2 miles (9 mins 18 3/5 secs)	119 lb
27th Oct	8 miles steady	Did not run ..	118 lb
28th Oct	Took a rest..		119½ lb
29th Oct	4 miles steady	8 miles slow..	118¼ lb
30th Oct	Sunday		119¾ lb
1st Nov	3 miles steady	10-mile trial (50 mins 55 secs)	118 lb
2nd Nov	2 miles fast..	5 miles steady	119 lb
3rd Nov	8 miles steady	4 miles fairly fast ..	119½ lb
4th Nov	Rested		119 lb

E

Race Performance

Miles	Min	Secs	Miles	Min	Secs	Miles	Min	Secs
¼	1	4 4/5	4¼	21	7 1/5	8¼	41	34 2/5‡
½	2	14 1/5	4½	22	23 1/5	8½	42	51 4/5‡
¾	3	28 2/5	4¾	23	39 2/5	8¾	44	8 3/5‡
1	4	44 1/5	5	24	55 4/5*	9	45	27 3/5‡
1¼	5	58 1/5	5¼	26	11 4/5	9¼	46	48 2/5‡
1½	7	12 3/5	5½	27	27 1/5	9½	48	5 4/5‡
1¾	8	28 3/5	5¾	28	48 1/5†	9¾	49	25 2/5‡
2	9	44 1/5	6	29	50 2/5‡	10	50	40 3/5‡
2¼	10	59 1/5	6¼	31	14 4/5‡	10¼	52	5 3/5‡
2½	12	14 3/5	6½	32	30 4/5‡	10½	53	30 3/5‡
2¾	13	30 3/5	6¾	33	48†	10¾	54	56 3/5‡
3	14	45 4/5	7	35	4 3/5†	11	56	23 3/5‡
3¼	15	1 3/5	7¼	36	22 1/5†	11¼	57	48 3/5†
3½	17	16 3/5	7½	37	39 2/5†	11½	59	10 4/5†
3¾	18	33 1/5	7¾	38	57 3/5†	11¾	60	32 1/5†
4	19	50 3/5	8	40	16‡			

* Scottish Record.
† World's Amateur Record.
‡ World's Amateur and Professional Record.

5

The Importance of being Zatopek

Emil Zatopek was born at Koprivnice, Moravia, on 19th September 1922. He was thus one of the earlier native citizens of the new Czechoslovak Republic set up after the First World War as one of the Succession States to the Austro-Hungarian Empire. He came of modest origins and at first entered industrial employment. He claims that he had no intention of becoming a runner. As a youth in occupied Czechoslovakia he was working in a shoe factory and housed in an industrial hostel with some 2,000 other apprentices, under a supervisor who was ambitious for social and athletic *kudos*. There was an annual local road-race which Zatopek managed to avoid until 1941, when his supervisor insisted on a full entry. Zatopek tried to take evasive action with a plea of unfitness, but since this failed he decided to run well to spite his supervisor. He came in second in the race and was invited to join the local club, which was an active one, and so became involved in the toils of competition – a fate he has never regretted.

Czechoslovakia, in its older form of Bohemia and Moravia, had a long tradition of physical education, going back to the 16th Century. The great educationalist, Jan Kominsky (Comenius) who dominated educational thought in the 17th Century (and was indirectly responsible for the founding of the Royal Society in England) strongly recommended physical training as an integral part of a balanced education. The tradition persisted and led to the creation in the 19th Century of the Bohemian Physical Training Association, SOKOL, which became associated with Czech national consciousness and therefore received a stimulus from the foundation of the new Czechoslovakian state in 1919.

This was, however, a nation-wide movement towards communal physical exercise and all-round physical fitness which did not produce any marked excellence in specialised branches of sport. Zatopek was in a sense fortunate in that standards were not particularly high in athletics, so that he could soon compete on equal terms with the best available talent, and at the same time there was enough interest in athletics to offer him encouragement when he showed his potential.

His first objective was the 1,500 metres. In 1943 he achieved his first big success when, as second string in a race for Moravia against Bohemia, he won and set up a new Czech record of 4 mins 1 sec.

Czechoslovakia did not then officially exist, except as a Government in exile in London. Slovakia was a Nazi puppet state and Bohemia and Moravia had been incorporated into Germany as a Protectorate. They were virtually a German colony and, with the rigours of war economy and an active resistance movement, living conditions were difficult. Nevertheless, the national tradition of physical training and athletic activity persisted, and was not hindered by the Germans, who no doubt regarded it as a safety-valve for young people in the occupied territory, and allowed local and regional organisations to continue.

Zatopek's performance was enthusiastically received among his own people as a national record. Although it was 15 seconds slower than Gundar Haegg's world record, it was much faster than the previous Czech national record, and it showed him his own potential. He was stimulated to direct his immense power of concentration and his active and original mind to the art and science of running. The result was a new approach to running which has revolutionised both training and tactics in distance running.

Zatopek is not powerfully built: even now in the middle forties, he is slim, even spare in figure. But he possessed immense stamina deriving partly from his tough physique, in which nothing is wasted, and partly from his unquenchable mental energy and will-power. He was temperamentally incapable of confining himself to the routine steady runs at an acceptable pace which had formed the staple of training in the past. He argued that this comfortable practice might well be good exercise for someone who merely wanted to keep generally fit, but that training would not yield competitive results in performance unless every session was a conscious effort at improvement. The logical answer was a great deal of work at full speed, aimed not merely at toning up the lungs and muscles but at constantly increasing the capacity for speed and endurance. This led him naturally to evolve his own system of interval training.

This form of training was not unknown, and it had its seeds in quite old methods, like cross-country running. The Swedes at Valedälen, as we have seen, had systematised it by alternating in their 'Fartlek', or 'pleasure-running', sprints and hill-climbs with easier stretches. The German coach and theoretician, Gerschler, had worked out a more precise system just before the war which has been used by many first-class athletes since. But owing to the war, nothing much had been heard of this and Zatopek owed nothing directly to it. In the autumn of 1945 he met Arne Andersson in Prague and listened carefully to his advice, but by then he had been practising and developing his own method for 3 years.

At the end of the war, Zatopek was drafted into the Army, where he found conditions of training – and rations – much better. He was posted to a garrison where the CO was interested in athletics and gave him encouragement, time for training, and leave for competition, of which he now got a good deal, mainly in national and international Army meetings. He decided to make the Army his career and entered the Military Academy as an Officer Cadet. He was commissioned 2nd Lieutenant in 1947 and married the daughter of the sympathetic CO – the Dana Zatopek who won the Women's Javelin event at the 1952 Olympic Games at Helsinki. She made her first – and record-breaking – throw just after he had won the 5,000 metres, and he likes to think that her elation contributed a few feet to her performance. He embodies their team-work in a monograph which suggests that her javelin contributes a stimulus to his speed, but in fact the marriage has been a remarkably happy partnership.

Interval training consists basically of running short bursts, flat out, alternating with intervals of slow running which enable the athlete to recover his oxygen-balance before the next burst. Since he never stops to rest completely, his training session is a *continuum*, so that he is actually covering a long distance to develop his stamina, and also training for speed. The most common or standardised form of interval training is lap-by-lap alternation on a 440 yards or 400 metres track, which allows runners to make

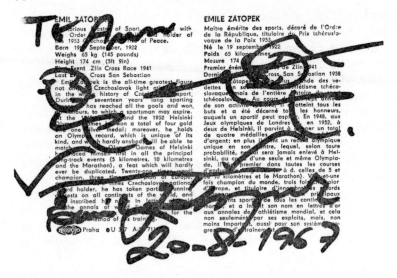

a considerable speed effort and take an extended recovery period. It is also convenient for checking speed and performance, as the quarter-mile or 400 metres lap is a conventional unit. Zatopek in his earlier years used a shorter and quicker system.

In 1943, when his aim was the 1,500 metres, Zatopek began with a pattern which he presented graphically (see illustration opposite).

This meant that he raced 100 metres, with an ease-off of 100 metres, raced another 100, with an ease-off of 200, raced 200, eased 200, raced another 200 with a 200 interval, raced 300 at the central point of the session, and then repeated the first section in reverse, so that he finished with a 100 metre sprint. The only variation in the palindrome was that he shortened his recovery intervals between the last three sprints, to simulate the pressure of the extended finishing burst.

The total of the speed-work in the first column was exactly 1,500 metres, but it had been run faster than would be possible without the jogged intervals. In his second formula he ran 1,600 metres in longer bursts of 200 metres twice, 400 twice and 200 twice, with corresponding intervals. The third pattern involved 10 times 200 metres with 200 metre intervals, varying to 10 times 100

$$1943$$

metres or 20 times 50 metres, and finishing with 6 times 400 metres, with 400 metre intervals. This added up to either 3,000 or 4,400 metres, excluding intervals.

When Zatopek stepped into top-class competition after the war, he moved up from his first love, the 1,500 metres, or metric mile, to 3,000, 5,000 and 10,000 metres. In the period when he was putting his training system into practice, he improved his 1,500 metres performance from 4 mins 13.9 secs in 1942 to 3 mins 59.4 in 1944. He did not improve on this in 1945, but in the following year he reduced his time to 3 mins 57.5, and in 1947, at his last serious attempt at the distance, he ran it in 3 mins 52.8 secs. This was $\frac{1}{5}$ second slower than Nurmi's best, and corresponds to just over 4 mins 10 secs for a mile. It should be remembered that Nurmi had a great deal more top-class competition at 1,500 metres and the mile.

But by 1945 Zatopek's eyes were set on the 5,000 metres, and in particular on matching Heino's performance. The effect of his interval training can best be measured by his progress at this distance:

5,000 *metres:*

1942...16 mins 25.0 secs
1943...15 mins 26.6 secs
1944...14 mins 55.0 secs
1945...14 mins 50.8 secs
1946...14 mins 25.8 secs
1947...14 mins 08.2 secs

The 1942 performance by a young man of 20 was no more than a creditable club performance which showed potential. The improvement in the 2 years to 14 mins 55 secs was remarkable considering that Zatopek was still (at the age of 22) making his own running with little coaching or opposition: the Czech record which he broke that year was 15 mins 14.8 secs. By comparison, the Finnish and Swedish runners who had had international competition before the war, with all the facilities involved, had not run a great deal faster. Måki won the European championship in 1938 with a performance of 14 mins 26.8 secs, and in 1939 put up a new world record at 14 mins 8.8 secs. In 1942, when Zatopek was at the start of his career, Gunder Haegg reduced this world record to 13 mins 58.2 secs. But these two runners and Heino, who beat Haegg at 5,000 metres but never ran faster than 14 mins 9.6 secs, were all seasoned international runners, who had been enjoying full facilities, coaching and competition for some years.

Zatopek, by contrast, in Nazi-occupied Czechoslovakia, was largely dependent on his own resources. When, still under the age of 24, he ran his first international race in the 1946 European Championships at Oslo, he finished fifth. His recollections of that race are amusing and typical. He was inclined to hero-worship Heino, as the heir of Nurmi and the decisive winner of the 10,000 metres race on the first day of the meeting. He had heard that Wooderson was the favourite in the 5,000 metres, but he could not believe it when he saw him. 'The elderly serious gentleman who stepped out on to the starting line had shorts which reached nearly down to his knees, and a pair of glasses on his nose.' In the light of this, he could not take Wooderson's reputed 'rocket finish' seriously and so probably dropped a couple of places, finishing in the fifth place, after the 'near-sighted professor' had rocketed past him.

Wooderson was indeed in this case the Professor, but Zatopek, coming, as it were, from nowhere, had made his mark on international running, finishing as he did a few metres behind Heino and 150 yards in front of the Belgian champion, Gaston Reiff. Thereafter, he began to pile on the heat.

In 1944 and 1945, he had been intensifying his 1943 schedule by doubling it for one week and halving it for the next, normally competing at the end of the lighter week. In 1946 he ran the double schedule every week. In 1947 he used a system of bursts of 400 metres alternating with recovery periods of 250 metres, which he repeated up to 20 times, with 'idling' intervals of 150 metres. This added up to the formidable total, excluding intervals, of 23.7 kilometres per session. He varied it by finding a course of soft ground with a curving contour measuring about 1,000 yards, on which he could run in both directions bursts of 100 metres, 120 metres, 100 metres, 150 metres and 120 metres, with idling intervals of about 100 metres. On the downhill bursts, he ran with long, leaping strides to intensify his effort. This was, incidentally, when he trained in Army boots, not so much to make his training more arduous, as to protect his ankles and avoid falls which might have caused injury. It was in 1947, during this phase of training, that he improved his 5,000 metres performance to 14 mins 8.2 secs, then the second fastest on record. It was not till 1954 that he finally beat Haegg's record with 13.57.2.

In 1948 he concentrated on track-work, with a schedule of 5 × 200 metres, 20 × 400 metres and 5 × 200 metres, in each case with a 200 metres interval. He began his bursts not at the starting point but at the end of the straight, just before the final bend, or at the beginning of the first bend, according to where his 'idling' interval brought him. This schedule gave him a total of 25 laps, or 10,000 metres (plus intervals). He had never run a 'straight' 10,000 metres, i.e., without idling intervals, until he competed at Budapest on 29th May, 1948, when he finished the course in 30 mins 28.4 secs. At his second attempt in Prague three weeks later, he achieved a time of 29 mins 37 secs, less than 2 seconds outside Heino's world record.*

Zatopek's third race over the distance was at the Olympic Games in London on 30th July, 1948. Most of the competitors suffered from the intense heat and humidity, but Zatopek (like Nurmi in Paris in 1924) did not seem to be affected. He set a fast pace which 'killed' Heino, who collapsed and retired after 4 miles. Even the French-Algerian, Alain Mimoun, who should have been inured to heat, was 300 yards behind Zatopek, in second place, and Abdulla ben Said, also of France, who secured sixth place, was a whole lap behind. This race marked the emergence of a new star of the magnitude of Paavo Nurmi.

Zatopek's ascendancy was not immediately apparent, because he was beaten 3 days later in the 5,000 metres event by the Belgian, Gaston Reiff, presumably through an error in pace-judgment. But the ascendancy soon became apparent. Since Nurmi's retirement in 1932, none of the many talented runners who had emerged to cut down his records at one distance or another had dominated the field in the way Nurmi in his time had done. It is true that the war interrupted the careers of many athletes, notably Wooderson; and that the Swedes and Finns, including Haegg, Andersson and Heino, who were in the ascendancy in 1939, were denied full international competition by the war. But the war was a greater handicap to Zatopek, who had to build up his career in Nazi-occupied Czechoslovakia. It is possible that Heino might have been dominant for 3 or 4 years, but this is hypothetical, because

* 29.35.4 at Helsinki, 25th August, 1944.

we do not know anything about the potential opposition which was swallowed up in the holocaust, and both Wooderson and Haegg were faster over 5,000 metres.

What is on record is that for the next 6 years Zatopek was in a class of his own. In, say, 1930, if Nurmi was entered for a race at his distance, no one would expect it to be won by anyone else, and the same thing applied to Zatopek between 1948 and 1954.

From May 1948 to July 1954, Zatopek ran 38 races at 10,000 metres and won them all. From October 1948 until June 1952 he won all his races at 5,000 metres. In the period from the London Olympic Games till his retirement in 1958, he set up 18 world records at distances from 5,000 to 30,000 metres, and was the first man to run more than 20 kilometres in an hour.* Almost all these records have been reduced, but one performance is almost certain to remain unique: that is, winning all the 3 distance races in one Olympiad – the 5,000 metres, 10,000 metres and marathon, at Helsinki in 1952.

Zatopek sometimes complains that it was not until he had done this that other athletes really took his training methods seriously and applied them; just as his friends in Moravia had laughed at him in his early days when he left them to pad around the track while he developed his interval training. Certainly after 1952 the standard of performance rose more steeply, and since Zatopek retired in January 1958 it has continued to rise. The last of his world records was overtaken in 1965 and his performances at 5,000 and 10,000 metres no longer appear in the first dozen of the world list. But his impact remains, just as Nurmi's still did when Zatopek was beginning to run. Its importance is not simply in his revolutionary use of the interval training system, towards which some other athletes were already feeling their way. His impact was more complex than this.

Zatopek's training methods did undoubtedly infuse a new element into the quest for speed and endurance. They did so primarily because he appeared when he did as the new star of the first magnitude, in the succession from George, Shrubb and Nurmi, the runners who stood out as unbeatable in their generation. He was able to demonstrate in person the value of his methods. This demanded personal qualities: the inexhaustible physical, mental and

* 20.052 kilometres = 12 miles, 810 yards.

moral energy; the sheer zest for competition and the exuberant enjoyment of racing which always communicated itself to spectators and to other competitors. Perhaps also an inbred gift of showmanship in a vivacious and challenging character. The combination of this natural talent, willingness to endure to the physical extreme, purposeful intelligence and vitality gave Zatopek his crucial position in the history of long-distance running. It made him the catalyst which released the elements of the great leap forward which is still in process.

Zatopek's version of interval training was also immensely important. After 1948 he intensified his training effort still more. He uses the formulae a) 5/40/5, b) 5/20/5, and c) 5/10/5, to describe his system. This means, respectively, a) 5 times 200 metres, plus 40 times 400 metres plus 5 times 200 metres in one session; b) 5 times 200 metres plus 20 times 400 metres plus 5 times 200 metres; c) 5 times 200 metres plus 10 times 400 metres plus 5 times 200 metres. In each case there was a 'jogging' interval of 200 metres between each fast run.

He wrote in response to an enquiry, just as this chapter was being completed: 'In the period 1950–53 my training was the same: 5/40/5, and my results were also the same: 5,000 metres in 14.03 mins, 10,000 metres in 29.02.6 mins in 1950 and 29.01.6 in 1953. Therefore in December 1953 I started to run more (up to 70 times 400 metres, with 100 metres jog in between) and after this I won the Sao Paolo Race on 31st December, 1953. In the year 1954 I ran up to 100 times 400 metres with 100 metres jog, and in the end of May I ran a world record for 5,000 metres (13.57.2 mins) and 10,000 metres (28.54.6 mins).'

After this his performance fell off and, with the additional handicap of a hernia operation, he confined himself to the Marathon at the Melbourne Olympics, finishing sixth.

However, his career was not finished. When he returned from Melbourne, he was invited to compete in the San Sebastian Cross-Country race in Spain, which is held in January. He declined for January, 1957, but promised to run the following year. He therefore resumed serious training during 1957. At this period he was concentrating on regaining speed, and for this purpose he selected a stretch of country with a slight incline of about 3%, which he used in both directions.

Zatopek did not resume serious competition at 10,000 metres, but he kept his promise to compete at San Sebastian, in January, 1958, and this was his last race.

There is not much doubt that if he had really tried he might still have improved on his own 10,000 metres performance. By then, however, he had decided to retire. He was 35 years old, and wanted to pursue his career in the Army and relax from the stringency of top-class competition, which he had endured for nearly twelve years.

Incidentally, in the letter quoted above, Zatopek also answered one or two personal enquiries. He wrote that although he occasionally ran 1,500 metres in his first class career, he never competed at a mile. He also added: 'I was really better at 10,000 metres than at 5,000 metres. In 1951, I was especially proud of my 20,000 metres record (59 mins 51.2 secs) and 1 hour race (20,052 metres).' [20 kilometres = 12 miles, 752 yards: 20,052 metres = 12 miles, 810 yards].

He regarded the Sao Paolo Road Race, of 7,300 metres, as a good criterion of form. His time of 20 mins 30 secs represents just about 14 mins for 5,000 metres.

The importance of Zatopek lies not in the list of records and the row of medals, but in the impact of his personality and approach on competitive running. The details quoted of his 1950–54 schedules add up to a formidable volume of work, but this is less significant than the method. He was always observing and checking his own performance, and the training was geared to correcting any weaknesses he found, and above all to adding an edge of real pace to his stamina.

In former times, including the post-Nurmi era of Finnish dominance, the general principal of long-distance training was that stamina could be developed by running further than the competitive distance at a slower speed; and pace could be developed by running a shorter distance at higher speed. To take an example: round about 1930 the AAA Four Miles Championship was still the most sought-after distinction for track distance runners outside the Olympic 5,000 and 10,000 metres contests. Kohlemainen won it in 1911, Backman of Sweden in 1919, Nurmi in 1922, Oehrn of Sweden in 1927 and Virtanen of Finland in 1930. It was abolished in 1932, when the 3 miles and 6 miles events were introduced to correspond with the Olympic distances, and the best performance had stood at 19 mins 32 secs by G. W. Hutson in 1913, despite Nurmi, Virtanen and the Swedish champions. Nurmi held the world record for 4 miles at 19 mins 15⅔ secs, but this was done in Finland not at the AAA Championships, where his performance was 19 mins 52⅔ secs.

An athlete training for this 4 miles race, and aiming at a performance of 19 mins 30 secs, would have run from 6 to 8 miles at a speed of 6 minutes per mile, perhaps three times a week. Once or twice a week he would have run about 2 miles at a pace faster than that required for a 4 miles in 19 mins 30 secs, i.e. as much under 9 mins 45 secs as he could get. He would also do some warming up before his runs, which might include a few bursts of up to 100 yards each, and, like Shrubb 30 years before him, he would finish each of his training spins with a finishing sprint of 100 yards or more.

This would represent a fair week's work, from Monday to Friday. On the Saturday there would be another run, or more probably a race over a shorter distance, such as a 1 mile handicap, or even a half-mile. In principal this was the pattern of training for this type of running, and the variation was in quantity rather than quality. Shrubb did more than George (although it should not be forgotten that George used to compete weekly through the summer, usually in two or more races on a Saturday, and ran a very full Cross-country schedule in the winter). Nurmi did more than Shrubb or than almost any of his contemporaries. Heino and Nurmi's other successors probably did more work than Nurmi, although this is not certain, since the Finns at that time tended to be somewhat secretive about their methods. Nurmi ran every day, usually twice a day, but his main work consisted of long runs at a speed well within his compass, together with long walks. The superiority of his training methods over those of his contemporaries lay not so much in the extra volume of work as in his practised judgment of pace – the stop-watch control which enabled him to spread his effort so evenly over the whole distance and so run more economically than his opponents.

In England the tradition of cross-country running, which, as we have seen, goes back to the Middle Ages, also formed a prototype of the Swedish *Fartlek*. It is a team-tradition in which clubs go out in packs, graded according to quality or taste. Members of the fast pack would cover perhaps 10 miles on a Saturday afternoon at varying speeds, sometimes racing one another over stretches of the course, and always having a full-speed run-in over the last half-mile or mile. In my own days we usually followed this by a fast walk on the Sunday of 20 miles or more at $4\frac{1}{2}$ to 5 miles an hour, and we did an evening road run in mid-week of perhaps 7 miles at a not too strenuous pace. This was a general pattern in hundreds of clubs round the country.

This tradition stood generations of British runners in good stead, and accounted for the high standard of stamina which characterised British distance-running. What it did not give was the sustained pace which the Finns and other Continental runners developed in the period from 1912 onwards. This was achieved by more intensive track-work and pace-judgment, which British runners were much slower to cultivate.

There was also the varying interpretation of amateur status, which was stricter in England than elsewhere and prevented athletes without private means from putting in the volume of work necessary to develop their potential fully. This explains the predominance of athletes from Oxford and Cambridge in British international teams up to the last war. The pattern of University life, which enabled athletes to spend every afternoon training on the very good tracks with which both Universities were equipped, gave these athletes a great advantage over those elsewhere who had to fit training and competition into the evenings and Saturday afternoons of a working week, often on tracks long distances away from home or work.*

Nurmi and many of his Continental rivals and successors were able to devote more time to training than any British athletes outside of Oxford and Cambridge, but his ascendancy was based on his more scientific approach to running, his stop-watch control of average pace. The legend that he always worked out his required performance arithmetically and ran his races without reference to his opponents will not stand up to close examination, as he often had to pull out everything he had in the last half lap, but he almost always succeeded. Nevertheless, his ability to win in the run-in, although he was never a sprinter and did not develop speed in training, was due to the pressure he put on his opponents by his even-paced running.

* After my first race against Nurmi, I grasped the idea of even-paced running, and used to time my laps with a stop-watch, but after coming down from Oxford I found it much more difficult to put this into practice after a full day's work.

It was true, and it still is, that an even performance is the most economical and therefore the optimum. But in competition at the top level – as Nurmi sometimes found – it is not always possible to plan and execute the theoretical optimum. Since his time, it has become more and more crowded at the top. This means that the real champions who, like Nurmi, are normally front-runners, have to vary their pace in order to spread-eagle the pursuit.

The importance of Zatopek's contribution to both training and competition methods was that he understood this (at first intuitively) and developed the means of winning under the new and tougher conditions. In doing so he taught others how to beat him and his records, but this is something he would be the last to regret. He believes in progress and, although he always fought tenaciously – and mostly successfully – to win his races or improve his records, he was well aware that every champion is a transient phenomenon. He held the field longer than anyone except Nurmi, at a time when it was getting immensely more difficult to hold it.

Towards the end of his career, Zatopek was overtaken by Chataway and Kuts at 5,000 metres and was defeated by Kovacs over 10,000 metres in 1954 – although he rapidly reversed this at the Berne European Games in the following month. One of the most comprehensive students of athletics, R. L. Quercetani, wrote of him: *

'As a champion distance runner, Zatopek had no weaknesses. In this respect he can be compared to Jesse Owens and Bobby Morrow among sprinters. A superlative solo runner (he received little or no help from others in his record attempts) he was also a clever tactician and an almost unbeatable finisher.'

It was this absence of weaknesses – this invulnerability – in a highly competitive age, which made Zatopek's contribution so important. It was not achieved merely by a natural superiority such as George, Shrubb and Nurmi exerted in their time. The natural ability was there, of course: not even the most brilliant of trainers has yet found a formula for making a silk purse out of a sow's ear. But by then, the natural ability was not enough. Zatopek developed his potential by his own outstanding intelligence and his inexhaustible energy and will-power. It was this dynamic approach to training, and its application to running methods, which revolutionised distance running. In other words,

* *A World History of Track and Field Athletics* (OUP 1964).

George or Shrubb, by their natural superiority could run anyone else into the ground, but this was no longer possible in Zatopek's time. He had to develop a technique with which to do it.

One of the most characteristic stories about him is his handling of the Helsinki marathon. He had already won the 5,000 and 10,000 metres races, but he had never run a full marathon course of 26 miles, 385 yards. He had done something equivalent in training sessions with intervals, lasting for as long as the 2 hours 20-odd minutes which he would need to win, but he had had no experience of judging the necessary pace. He has recorded his solution.*

'In the end I dropped all tactical considerations and decided to keep my eye on the best competitor. The papers wrote that the favourite was Jim Peters and that his number was 187. When we took our places in front of the grandstand, I caught sight of a runner with his number, and I immediately went and asked if he really was Peters. After all, there is nothing like making sure. If the newspapers had got it wrong and I had "tailed" somebody else by mistake, who knows what the outcome would have been?'

Zatopek recounts elsewhere that Peters started off surprisingly fast and was 150 yards ahead when they got out of the stadium. He decided to catch him up gradually, which he did after about 10 miles, taking the Swede, Jansson with him. Jansson flagged after 25 kilometres and Zatopek kept going as best he could for the last 10 miles and won in the new Olympic record time of 2 hours 23 mins 3.2 secs, 2½ minutes in front of Gorno of Argentina, who beat Jansson for second place.

This was a typical example of Zatopek's intelligent empiricism in a new situation. He always ran to win, and this meant using the tactics which would beat his opponents, and drawing on his astonishing reserves built up by his almost masochistic training system. He said (in a recent speech in Montreal) about the finish of the race:

'Alone, my mouth parched and more and more tired out with every kilometre I staggered along, peering out over the heads of the spectators whether the Olympic Stadium wasn't in view yet.

I was only brought out of my trance by the ceremonial fanfares as I ran through the Marathon Gateway. People were standing up from their seats, waving to me and calling out greetings

* *XVII Olympiad, Rome 1960*, ed. Harold Abrahams, Cassell 1960, p. 55.

F

with joy. And I was so very grateful to them, though I didn't manage to do more than to take great care not to stumble and make a fool of myself. In the goal I was overjoyed with the sudden, wonderful feeling of being able to stand on my own feet and having to run no more.'

At the end of the marathon no one is very conscious of anything much, but in this case the pattern for victory had been set in the earlier stages while Zatopek was still able to pit his judgment against his adversaries, and, as he had calculated, it was then only a question of holding out. This was quintessential Zatopek.

6

The Mile and the Marathon

(1) Mile

All distance runners are concerned at some stage with the mile, and almost all begin their careers with it. Every schoolboy who catches the distance running bug first sets his heart on the mile. The distance-pace type of runner whose peak is at 3 miles or 5,000 metres – Ladoumègue, Wooderson, Haegg, Chataway – must be in the top flight over a mile: of these four, Chataway, who competed least seriously over the mile, actually recorded the fastest time, as he was among the earliest runners to break the 4-minute barrier. Nowadays, even runners whose best distance is 6 miles or 10,000 metres must be somewhere near the 4-minute class.

The mile has a great history and mystique. It was the *mille passus* (in the plural, *milia passuum*) by which the Roman legions measured their inexhaustible marches across the known world. Their *passus* was a double stride, and the single stride was just under 2 ft. 5 in. This made the *mille*, 1,611 yards, or 1,450 metres. The stride seems short, but the legionaries carried a great deal besides their weapons and armour: 3 days' rations, trenching tools, axes, saws, mess-tins and even a wicker basket for transporting earth to build fortifications. The Jewish historian Josephus, describing the Roman army in the 1st Century AD said that the infantryman was as heavily laden as a mule. So a standard day's march of 24 *milia* – or 22 English miles – in 8 hours was quite good going.

Most European countries where the Romans penetrated have their mile, but the distance varies enormously from a kilometre to the old German mile which was nearly 7 kilometres. In England, when athletic competition in its modern form was revived, it was natural that a mile race should become popular. The Romans had installed mile-posts (*miliaria*) all over their empire, including Britain and, although these fell out of use in the Middle Ages, they were restored – registering the rather longer standard English mile – in the 18th Century, when road transport was systematised. Milestones (*bornes milaires*) were also general in France before the Revolution. The traditional French mile was 1,000 *toises*, which was just over 2,000 yards (a *toise* was 76 inches) but lineal measures varied wildly in France. After the Revolution, the milestones were standardised as *bornes kilomètriques* and spread all over the Napoleonic Empire along the great network of strategic roads Napoleon built.*

The English mile of 8 furlongs (or furrow-lengths) was a natural and challenging distance: fast enough to be exciting, and long enough to sustain excitement. When athletic sports were organised on grass tracks in the 19th Century, the mile was already traditional, and the 4 quarter-mile laps fitted conveniently on football or cricket grounds. When cinder-tracks were built in the second half of the century, the 440 yards lap was an obvious standard (although up to the last war there were grounds, such as the Oxford track at Iffley Road and the Cambridge one at Fenners', with laps of one-third of a mile and the Stade Jean-Bouin in Paris was, with typical French illogic, 450 metres).

The earliest mile races of which we have any credible records were run in not much under 5 mins,† but by the late sixties runners broke the 4 mins 30 secs mark. Walter Chinnery was timed at 4.29$\frac{4}{5}$ at Fenners' in 1868, and by 1875 Walter Slade had done 4.24$\frac{1}{2}$. When W. G. George came to the fore about 1880, there was already an outstanding middle-distance runner, an American, Laurence E. Myers from Virginia, who ran a good deal in England. He first broke 50 secs for the 440 yards, and 3 times recorded 1.55$\frac{2}{5}$ for the half-mile. He beat George at 880 yards, but could not stay with him at a mile.

In 1882 George achieved 4.19$\frac{2}{5}$ at the AAA. Championships at Stamford Bridge, and 2 years later brought the amateur record

---

* The French revolutionaries introduced the metre and kilometre as arbitrary standard measures (just as they changed the names of the calendar months). Napoleon's campaigns imposed the kilometre on a large part of Europe.
† Chapter I. ii.

down to $4.18\frac{2}{5}$. He then gave up his amateur status, as we have seen, to be able to run against the only man who could extend him, and accomplished 4 mins $12\frac{3}{4}$ secs in 1885. It would be difficult to overrate this performance. It could not rank as an amateur record, but it was professional only technically, and should be included, historically considered, in the development of mile running.

George's amateur record was lowered to $4.17\frac{4}{5}$ in 1893 by an American, Thomas Conneff. In 1895 an Englishman, Frederick Bacon, recorded 4.17 at the AAA Championships, but in the same year Conneff brought the record down to $4.15\frac{3}{5}$ in New York. Joe Binks set up a British amateur record of $4.16\frac{4}{5}$ in 1902, but Conneff's world record stood until 1911, when it was cut to $4.15\frac{2}{5}$ by another American, John Paul Jones. But George's record was not touched by amateur or professional until 1915 when another fine American runner, Norman Taber, clocked $4.12\frac{3}{5}$. Since he had the benefit of a watch calibrated in fifths of a second, it is open to doubt whether his time was actually faster than George's, measured in quarters of a second. As we have seen, the race was a contrived handicap which would not pass contemporary rules. In 1923 Paavo Nurmi settled the point by returning $4.10\frac{2}{5}$ in a race in Stockholm in which he was in front most of the way.

There the mile record remained until Ladoumègue brought it down to $4.09\frac{1}{5}$ in 1931. Then came a spate of fast British milers, J. F. Cornes, Reginald Thomas, and Jack Lovelock, a New Zealander who did his best running in England. Lovelock made the next break in 1933, when he beat the fine American miler, Bill Bonthron, in 4.07.6. In 1934 another fine American runner, Glenn Cunningham, reached 4.06.7. Lovelock beat Cunningham in the 1936 Olympic 1,500 metres, setting up a new world record.

By this time another Englishman, Sidney Wooderson, who had been incapacitated at the 1936 Olympic Games, had reached his prime, and in 1937 lowered the mile record to 4.06.4, although this again was in a contrived handicap race. The stage was then set for the Swedish school to make their inroads and by 1945 Haegg had brought the record down to 4.01.4. He and Andersson at that point lost their amateur status: they had done an immense amount of sponsored running and had certainly broken the rules. They were both very close to the 4 mins and, given another season of competition, might well have broken it.

Even so, they had made a remarkable advance. George's record of 4 mins 12¾ had stood from 1885 until 1915, when it was scarcely more than equalled by Norman Taber, and so till 1923, when Nurmi reduced it to 4.10⅖. The improvement in 38 years was 2¼ secs, or 0.8 of 1 per cent. Up to 1937, after another 14 years, the reduction was 4 secs, or 1.6 per cent. Haegg and Andersson in the next 8 years knocked 5.1 seconds off, that is, just under 2.1 per cent.

For the next 7 years no advance was made: no one ran a mile in less than 4 mins 1.4 secs. But towards the end of 1952 and in 1953, John Landy of Australia, Wes Santee of America and Roger Bannister of Britain all registered about 4 mins 2 secs. Bannister, a highly intelligent athlete, then a medical student, planned his training carefully, with the advice of the Austrian coach, Franz Stampfl, and by 1954 was prepared to attempt to break 4 minutes for the mile. This he achieved in May 1954 in a race at Oxford in which two other outstanding Oxford athletes, C. J. Chataway and C. Brasher were competing.* His time of 3.59.4 was a great athletic sensation, because he had broken the 'sound barrier' of 4 minutes. 6 weeks later the Australian John Landy cut the record to 3.57.9 at Turku, Finland, and in the same race set up a new 1,500 metres record of 3.41.8.

In August of that year Bannister and Landy met at Vancouver in the Commonwealth Games, and Bannister won what has been called the 'mile of the century' by ⅘ of a second in 3.58.8.

In the next few years there was a wealth of talent in the mile, and performances under 4 minutes became frequent. In London in 1955 the Hungarian, Roszavolgyi won a race in which Chataway and Hewson of England were also inside 4 minutes. In 1958 at Dublin Herbert Elliott of Australia won a mile race in 3.54.5 in which 4 other runners were inside 3.58.6. By 1966 more than a 100 runners had beaten 4 minutes, and the record was down to 3.51.3. Thus in 21 years there was an improvement of 10.1 seconds in the mile record, or just over 4 per cent. In the previous 22 years the improvement was about 2.8 per cent, and in the previous 38 years only 0.8 of 1 per cent.

The new factor was certainly interval training. Bannister probably did less volume of work than George or Nurmi, but he

* Bannister, Chataway and Brasher had by then all left Oxford, and were representing an AAA team against Oxford.

trained at a faster pace. Interval training is explained in detail in Chapter VII. Briefly, it consists of alternating intervals of running at full speed with intervals of slower running, in one continuous training session, and this has proved immensely effective in enabling runners at 1 mile and upwards to sustain higher speeds over longer distances.

The most remarkable phenomenon in mile-running is the young American, Jim Ryun, who was born in 1947, and had set up decisively new records for the mile and 1,500 metres before he was 21 years old. Another American, Jim Grelle, at the age of 30 had run more miles inside 4 minutes than anyone else in the world, but he could not stay with Ryun.

In 1966 the *Daily Mail* newspaper set up a computer and fed into it all the data to find out the likely trend of performances at the mile. The machine said that the mile record would come down to 3 mins 52 secs by 1970, and could go just below 3 mins 48 secs by 1980. A few days later, Jim Ryun, at the age of 19, ran a mile in 3 mins 51.3 secs. In June 1967, he ran a mile in 3 mins 51.1 secs, and shortly before that he had run 1,500 metres in 3 mins 33.1 secs, which is equivalent to a little under 3 mins 49 secs, for a mile. All this was part of his build-up for the 1968 Olympic Games, so the computed record of 3 mins 48 secs for 1980 is very likely to be established before 1970.

So much for computers. Jim Ryun will be just 21 when he goes to compete at Mexico City – most probably in the 800 metres and 1,500 metres. He is tall and long-legged (6 feet 2 inches 1.87 metres) and is called by his friends 'the Stork in Shorts'. At the age of 19 he ran 2 miles in 8 mins 25.2 secs, beating the great African runner, Keino. He has incredible speed, and it is said of him that he can outsprint anyone in a mile, and that, unless the pace in the first 3 laps is fairly stiff, he is capable of a last lap of 52 seconds. Keino has a very fast finish: in the race in which Ryun set up his 1,500 metres record, there was a relatively slow start, Ryun went into the lead, then Keino went in front, and Ryun made his 'strike' about 350 yards from the finish and beat Keino by at least 30 yards.

Ryun has an athletic scholarship at the Kansas University, which means that he has a grant over and above his academic bursary, which enables him to pursue athletics in his vacations, instead of working in a store or a factory, as most American students do to keep themselves at College. He also has relatives in Colorado, so that he is able to spend a good deal of time exercising at an altitude of about 7,000 feet, which improves his performance at sea-level, and will certainly help to boost his performance at Mexico City. He has been coached by one of the best American coaches, Bob Timmons, who also coached that great runner, Archie San Romano, who did a 4 mins 10 secs, mile while still at school.

Ryun has been accused of being withdrawn and introspective, but this is not true. He likes to take 3 or 4 days rest before a big race, and makes himself scarce. This does not endear him to newspapermen. Christopher Chataway described him as 'lively, high-spirited and intelligent', and possessed of a great fund of confidence and will-power. Ryun does about 45 minutes of 'easy' running every morning, sometimes more, running as far as 12 miles, and about 90 minutes of interval training in the afternoon.

Jim Ryun is a very good prospect for the 800 metres and 1,500 metres at Mexico City. If, after that, he turns his attention to the 5,000 metres, we shall see some very interesting results. But if he never runs again, he will go down to history as a legendary figure in the running of the mile.

The development of performance in mile running is a story in itself, but it has also been immensely important in raising the sights for the longer races. The mile was always the threshold of long-distance running and therefore the pace-setter for the next distances – 3 miles and 5,000 metres. When the pace of these was 'hotted up' by mile performances, they passed on the new conceptions of pace to the next category of 6 miles and 10,000 metres.

(2) Marathon

The marathon is a romantic accident. The Greeks never competed over more than about 3 miles, but the Victorian revivers of the Olympic Games were captivated by the association of the name. There was Byron's romanticism:

'The mountains look on Marathon
And Marathon looks on the sea.'

And there was the fascination of 19th Century archaeology, Schliemann's Troy and the excavations at Delphi during the 1890's which laid bare the most sacred city of Classical Greece.

The marathon legend, according to Herodotus, was that when the Persians landed at Marathon in 490 BC the Athenians sent a runner, called Pheidippides, to ask the Spartans for help, and that he ran the 160 miles between Athens and Sparta in less than 48 hours. According to Plutarch, (who lived about 4 centuries later, whereas Herodotus was born 5 years after the battle and wrote some 40 years later) an Athenian called Eucles returned from abroad after the Athenian Army had marched out to Marathon to meet the Persians. He ran the 24 miles from Athens in time to fight in the battle, then ran back to Athens to announce the victory, and fell dead – whether of wounds or heart-failure is not clear. An unkinder tradition represents him as a deserter. However dubious the legend, the founders of the modern Olympic Games were determined to celebrate the great Athenian victory, so they included a race from Marathon to Athens in the first Olympiad.

The distance was 40 kilometres (24 miles 1,500 yards) and the race was won by a Greek, Spiridiou Louis, in 2 hrs 58 mins 50 secs and 5 of the first 6 finishers were Greek. Since then only one Greek has ever been placed in the first 6. At the second Olympiad, at Paris in 1900, the course was just over 25 miles and French runners finished first, second and fourth.*

In 1904, at St Louis, the course reverted to 40 km. and Americans finished first, second, third and sixth. The winner took 3 hrs 28 mins 53 secs. The marathon at the London Olympiad of 1908 was also won by an American, John Hayes.† It was noteworthy in two respects: the course of 42.195 kilometres or 26 miles 385 yards was the distance afterwards agreed on as the standard marathon – although not until 1924 in Olympic contests. Kohlemainen had to run 42,750 metres (26 miles 990 yards) at Antwerp in 1920 which makes his time of 2 hours 32 mins 35.8 secs the best performance until 1936.

The present standard of 26 miles 385 yards derives from the

* The rather devious course around the tram-lined suburbs of Paris may have favoured the natives. The winner, M. Théato, was a baker's roundsman.
† Time: Dorando 2 hours 54 minutes 46.4 seconds. Hayes 2 hours 55 minutes 18.4 seconds.

further accident that the course chosen, from the Windsor Great Park to the White City Stadium was 26 miles plus the distance of 385 yards from the entrance of the Stadium to the finishing post in front of the Royal Box, which was added when it was known that King Edward VII and Queen Alexandra would be there.

Until 1920, when Kohlemainen took it in hand, the marathon was much more romantic than scientific. At St Louis, where the official distance tallied with the original Athenian course, the first man to finish was afterwards found to have had a lift in an automobile for about 10 miles of the course and was disqualified. This was one of the first impacts of the Internal Combustion Engine. The actual winner is known to have had several injections of strychnine during the last few miles, but was not disqualified since there were not then any rules about the use of drugs in athletics.

At London in 1908 there was another colourful incident when Dorando Pietri, the tough little Italian runner who reached the Stadium first, collapsed and was helped up by officials and first-aid workers. He staggered on towards the Royal Box, falling occasionally and finally collapsed just in front of the tape. He was helped over the finishing line and promptly disqualified by the judges. John Hayes of the United States had meanwhile entered the Stadium and finished as winner about half a minute later.

The Dorando incident aroused enormous public sympathy. A special cup was presented by Queen Alexandra to the courageous loser (Arthur Conan Doyle, the inventor of Sherlock Holmes, was the instigator of this gesture). Even in the 1920s the term 'to do a Dorando' was still in popular use to signify collapsing in front of the tape. The race stimulated great interest in marathon-running in the United States, and both John Hayes and Dorando Pietri became professionals and ran a number of marathons during the next 12 months in America, in which Dorando usually beat Hayes, but was himself beaten by a Canadian-Indian, called Thomas Longboat.

By the 1912 Olympic Marathon, at Stockholm, marathon running was becoming more systematic, and the Scandinavians had begun to take an interest. The course at Stockholm worked out at 40.2 kilometres – 200 metres longer than the original Athens course. The road was swept and cleared of traffic. The eldest of the Kohlemainen brothers, Tatu, took the lead in the earlier stages, but faded out. The race was won by K. K. McArthur of South Africa, with another South African, Gitsham, second, followed by 2 Americans, a Canadian and a Swede in 6th place. The time was much faster than anything before. McArthur finished in 2 hours 36 mins 54.8 secs, Gitsham was about 1 minute behind and the 6th man, S. Jacobsson of Sweden, recorded 2 hours 43 mins 24 secs.

Even allowing for the extra mile and a quarter which Hayes and Dorando Pietri had to run in London, Jacobsson was still more than 5 mins faster.

In the 1920 Olympiad at Antwerp there was a further sharp improvement. Hannes Kohlemainen finished in 2 hours 32 mins 35.8 secs with Lossman of Esthonia only 13 seconds behind. When we consider that this course was 42.75 kilometres – 2.75 kilometres longer than at Athens, and 550 metres longer than the London course – which has since become the standard – the performance is quite remarkable. If we subtract the extra 550 metres at the average speed, Kohlemainen's equivalent time for the standard marathon distance would be inside 2 hrs 30 mins 30 secs.

After Kohlemainen, the marathon race began to be thought of in terms of 2½ hours, rather than 3 hours, and marathon runners began to systematise their pace-judgment.

In 1929 H. W. Payne established what was regarded as the world's best marathon performance, when he ran from Windsor to Stamford Bridge, London, in 2 hrs 30 mins 57⅗ secs, and this was not bettered until the Japanese runner, K. Son, achieved 2 hrs 29 mins 19.2 secs at the Berlin Olympiad in 1936. Unlike track records, marathon performances cannot be compared exactly, because the courses vary – the Windsor to London course included some fairly stiff gradients which Berlin, Antwerp and most other courses do not have* – but Harry Payne's fine performance in 1929 was not actually as fast as Kohlemainen's in 1920, which did not however involve climbing.

Harry Payne had no academic education beyond elementary school, but he was a man of great native intelligence who educated himself generally and applied his brains to running. Even gas-

---

* The Berlin course, absolutely flat on a good surface, was the fastest ever until Tokyo.

poisoning in the First World War did not interfere with his athletic career. He was incidentally a vegetarian, but this was due to his own (and his wife's) principles, not to any dietetical theory of training. He did a great deal of cross-country running at Club and international level and competed frequently as part of his training. He was a good track runner at 4 miles but frequently competed at 1 mile, or even less, to develop pace. He believed in even-paced running and a steady start. He used to say at the start of a 10 miles or marathon race, when most competitors were going off very fast, 'Let them go: they'll all come back', and so indeed they usually did, as he overhauled them with his unflagging pace, which seemed very fast in the second half of a marathon and was in fact a little faster than his speed in the earlier stages.

Paavo Nurmi ran 2 hours 22 minutes over a course of just under 25 miles (40.2 kilometres) in 1932,* but was not able to compete in that year's Olympic event, which was won by J. C. Zabala of Argentina in 2 hrs 31 mins 36 secs, with Ferris of Great Britain 19 seconds behind. K. Son of Japan† improved on this in 1936, but it was not till 1952 that Zatopek made a radical improvement with 2 hrs 23 mins 3.2 secs at Helsinki.

In Zatopek's era, a British marathon runner, James Peters, had been training systematically and had returned several very fast times. In June 1952 he won the British marathon championship in 2 hrs 20 mins 4.2 secs, a new world record. At Helsinki the following month he misjudged his pace and had to retire.‡ In 1953 he improved on his own record with 2 hrs 18 mins 40 secs. He ran his fastest marathon, also in the British championships, in 1954: 2 hrs 17 mins 39.4 secs. Unfortunately he again misjudged his race later that year when he should have won the Commonwealth Games Marathon at Vancouver. He was vulnerable to high temperatures, and this race was run on a very hot day over a difficult course. Peters could have won comfortably but he attempted to get inside 2 hrs 20 mins. He reached a point just outside the Stadium in 2 hrs 19 mins, but was finally exhausted by a short gradient there and tottered into the Stadium in a state of collapse. He fell several times during the last lap and was picked up and carried away after he had literally crawled

* This corresponds to about 2 hours 29 minutes for the full distance.
† He was actually born in Korea.
‡ p. 81.

over the finishing line for the track events, which was a few yards short of the finishing post for the marathon. The next runner, who entered the stadium 15 minutes later, but still under control, was therefore the winner. Peters was advised to give up competition, and did so.

This sad experience illustrates the immense strain imposed by the marathon, which is not comparable with anything else in athletics. In a book to which he later contributed, with two other distinguished athletes,* Peters stresses the enormous importance of the 'last 6 miles 385 yards'. There is a vast difference between even a 20-mile race and a marathon. The extra distance, its arbitrary length, and the absence of any routine measurement, like the lap on the track, makes pace judgment extremely difficult. The impact of the unyielding road surface on feet and legs is an added strain which a track runner does not undergo.

Peters did not unfortunately follow his own excellent advice on marathon running. He stresses the importance of running at an even pace 'within yourself' and avoiding too fast a pace in the early stages. He also advises finding another competitor to use a pace-setter. But in his two major international marathon races, at Helsinki and Vancouver, he insisted on setting his own pace, out in front. In the first he was used by Zatopek as pace-maker. In the second he set himself a dangerously and unnecessarily fast pace which exhausted him just a few hundred yards before the finish.

In his training schedules Peters followed the older pattern of Shrubb and Nurmi, although Zatopek and the Scandinavians had already demonstrated the value of interval training. He ran at even speeds, on average about 10 miles a day, with very occasional longer distances up to 20 miles, but did not run the full marathon distance except in competition, once or twice a year. Although his mileage looks impressive – from September 1950 to May 1951, for instance, he covered over 1,200 miles – he actually did very little speed-work, except in competition, and none of this at short distances. Peters did a great deal of cross-country running, but in competition he mainly concentrated on the Marathon. That he never won a big international race was partly due to the exigencies of the Marathon, but partly also to his

* *Modern Middle and Long-Distance Running,* by Peters, Johnston and Edmundson (Nicholas Kaye, 1957).

failure to learn from the experience of other athletes – notably Zatopek.

Peters was (and is) an intelligent man and a qualified pharmacist, but, like many other English distance-runners, he did not sufficiently apply his intelligence to training and running, with the intensity so many Continental, American and Australasian athletes have devoted. He was also, perhaps, a victim of the excessive 'amateurism' of the British attitude to athletics. In 1954 he continued to do a full-time job as a pharmacist and took his two weeks annual leave just before the Vancouver Games for his final burst of training, into which he probably put too much effort in too short a time.

It was a sad thing that this very fine athlete did not win the top prizes of which he was capable. While he was competing, a strong school of marathon runners grew up in the Soviet Union, where the conditions of training for this arduous race are easier to come by. By careful selection and training, a group of high power marathon runners was built up. Two of them performed impressively at the 1954 European Games, although they were just beaten by the Finnish champion, Veikko Karvonen.

The 1956 Olympic marathon at Melbourne was won by the Algerian Alain Mimoun Okacha, representing France. In 1958 the Russian, Sergey Popov won in the European Games from in front in the devastating time of 2 hrs 15 mins 17 secs. It began to look as though the centre of gravity in marathon performance had shifted back to Europe. But in 1960 a new and unexpected challenge arose. At the Rome Olympiad the Ethiopian runner, Abebe Bikila, won with apparent ease in 2 hrs 15 mins 16.2 secs, with Rhadi ben Abdesselem, of Morocco, second, and Magee of New Zealand third. The European champion, Popov, was fifth. It was the fastest marathon race to date, with 15 competitors finishing inside Zatopek's existing Olympic record.

In the late twenties of this century, there was a strong upsurge of marathon running in Japan, which culminated in the victory of Kitei Son at Berlin in 1936, with a fellow-countryman, Shoryu Nan, third. The Japanese lost their ascendancy following the last war, but after 1960 they again came to the forefront. Toru Terasawa achieved a time of 2 hrs 16 mins 18.4 secs in winning the Asahi marathon in Japan in 1962. This was also a very fast race. Nakao of Japan was only 35 seconds behind, and Kimihara, of Japan, Edelen of the USA and Kantorek of Czechoslovakia were all inside 2 hours 19 minutes.

In the following year, Terasawa won another marathon race in 2 hrs, 15 mins 15.8 secs – $\frac{2}{5}$ of a second faster than Abebe's Olympic record – and 9 other runners in the race finished in less than 2 hrs 20 mins. Abebe Bikila was beaten in a marathon race in Boston in the following year, and no European or American had got within 5 minutes of Terasawa's time. Thus, although marathon performances on different courses are not strictly comparable, it looked as though the Japanese runners would more or less monopolise the Tokyo marathon in 1964.

In the event, Abebe Bikila upset all the form by winning again in the astonishing time of 2 hrs 12 mins 11.2 secs. 4 minutes behind him was Basil Heatley of Great Britain. A Japanese runner, K. Tsuburava, of whom little had been heard, was third, with Kilby of Britain, Sütö of Hungary and Edelen of the United States (who was actually then living and training in Britain) fourth, fifth and sixth. Kimihara of Japan was eighth and Teresawa only fifteenth.

This was certainly a marathon in depth, for, of the 58 runners who finished, 18 were inside 2 hours 25 minutes and Pystynen of Finland who came in twentieth was only a split second outside 2 hours 26 minutes. It outdid even the brilliance of the Rome marathon.

It is clear that in this period, 1960 to 1964, the marathon really came of age. One significant point is the large number of competitors in the Tokyo marathon who had already run in the 10,000 metres. Ron Clarke, who finished 9th in the marathon, had been narrowly beaten into third place in the 10,000 metres in a tremendously fast last lap, and had also competed in the 5,000 metres. Others who were also among the first 20 finishers in both the 10,000 metres and the marathon were W. Mills, USA, Mamo Wolde, Ethiopia, Tsuburaya, Japan, R. Hill, Great Britain and J. Sütö, Hungary.

Zatopek's brilliantly improvised act of pace-judgment at Helsinki, based on adjustment to the speed of the likeliest winner, would no longer have worked. Abebe again made his own pace and no one could stay with him.

What sort of pace is now necessary to win a marathon in this class? Up to 1952, when Zatopek brought the time down to 2 hrs 23 mins, and Peters achieved 2 hrs 20 mins, a time around $2\frac{1}{2}$ hours was good enough to win almost any marathon. Only K. Son at Berlin in 1936 had beaten $2\frac{1}{2}$ hours, and then only by 40 secs. This represents as near as nothing a rate of 5 mins 40 secs per mile. If we divide the distance into 4 stretches of 10,000 kilometres plus a fraction of 2.195 kilometres, we get an average of 33 mins 10 secs for each 10,000 metres, when a marathon runner does 2 hrs 30 mins.

An analysis of the intermediate stages of the 3 fastest marathons run before Ababe Bikila's Tokyo performance, by Popov, Bikila (at Rome) and Terasawa, all about 2 hrs 15 mins 16 secs, shows considerable uniformity of pace.

	Popov	.Bikila	.Terasawa
(1)	31.45	31.07	32.43
(2)	30.45	31.32	32.52
(3)	32.05	31.50	31.14
(4)	33.08	34.04	31.21
*Fraction	7.38	6.43.2	7.05.8
	[2 hrs. 15 mins 17]	[2 hrs 15 mins 16.2]	[2 hrs 15 mins 15.8]

The average speed per 10,000 metres is almost exactly 32 minutes. Both Popov and Bikila were slowed up in their fourth leg through having run well inside average for the first 30 kilometres. Terasawa, who achieved marginally the overall fastest time, was the most even-paced and ran the second half of the race about 3 minutes faster than the first. This was a development of Harry Payne's technique.

The target speed of 3 minutes 12 seconds per kilometre was raised (or lowered) by Bikila at Tokyo to under 3 minutes 8 seconds. The marathon will soon move to a target of 2 hours, which means 2 mins 51 secs a kilometre, or 4 mins 34 secs per mile. It is unfortunate that the combination of romanticism and royalty fixed the marathon at the odd distance of 26 miles 385 yards. The founder-fathers of the Olympic Games would have

---

* These figures are not quite accurate (as some simple arithmetic will show) because they were only approximate readings, ignoring fractions of seconds, but they are near enough for comparison. Bikila's fourth leg and his fraction were probably wrongly divided by up to 30 seconds. The source is Quercetani (op. cit. p. 80).

How to win a Marathon and relax: Abebe Bikila, Tokyo 1964. Time 2 hours 12 min. 11.2 sec.

Peter Snell beats George Kerr: Commonwealth half-mile, Perth 1962

done much better to settle for the tidy distance of 40 km., which could be divided into multiples of 10,000 metres and of 5,000 metres. This would have made it easier for the runners to calculate their pace, and much easier for reporters and critics to compare performances.

Nevertheless, there is some residual romance in the running of this odd distance, together with the increasing use of scientific methods, which will almost certainly bring the best performance down to 2 hours within the next 5 years. The marathon, in spite of its odd genesis, is like the mile in that it touches the imagination more than any of the metric distances. The 'Four-minute' mile was, so to speak, logically imaginative (as Matthew Arnold wrote of the power of 'imaginative reason') because it involved running four 440 yard laps of 60 seconds and somewhere under-cutting them: a 'four-minute mile', with typical British illogic, means the opposite of what it says – a mile run in less than 4 minutes.

The marathon, since Zatopek's experiment in 1952, has moved a very long way. It still has far to go – and this is not meant as a play on words. Since Bikila emerged in Rome in 1960, the marathon has got down to business, and performances will go on improving. But from the beginning of the modern Olympics, when it was dreamed up, it has always been the great climax, whether the winner took about 3 hours, or not much more than 2 hours to complete the course. The sheer fortitude involved in doing this has always been recognised as the high-spot of athletic competition. And the marathon is in a class of its own. I recall an Olympic marathon runner saying: 'After about 15 miles you get into a state in which your legs feel like wooden stumps and you are carrying on inside a kind of fog which you take along with you.' When I afterwards ran a marathon, I understood exactly what he meant.

But, irrespective of arithmetically considered performances, the marathon has always commanded great respect, because those who finish at all at this distance must have a lot of guts. The marathon race at the first modern Olympiad in Athens in 1896 was the high point of the meeting – not only because it was won by a Greek after Americans had won most of the track and field events, but for its own sake. This tradition has continued. The marathon is always staged as the last race and climax of every

G

Olympiad, and the winner is received accordingly. When Zatopek won in 1952, after having won the 5,000 and 10,000 metres races, he was cheered more loudly than anyone in the history of the Games.

This enthusiasm is – quite rightly – evoked by anyone who can take on this most exacting of athletic efforts and somehow finish in front. This is really the climax. When sports reporters begin to write about a 'two-hour' marathon (meaning the opposite) the science of athletics will be near fulfilment.

7
From Zatopek to Clarke

Zatopek, who still takes a very close interest in running, regards Ron Clarke as the culmination to date of distance running. Clarke said on one occasion that he would like to take part in an anachronistic race between himself, Nurmi, Kuts, Zatopek and one or two other former champions, all at their peak, and that he would not be at all confident of winning it, although statistically his own performances would put him well in front. He would not be surprised if either Nurmi or Zatopek might beat him.

His argument was that great runners will always win their races, and run as fast as they think they can, but their record performances will always be conditioned by their target. He is also impressed by Nurmi's ability, whenever his planned schedule proved insufficient, to pull out whatever extra was needed: as he did in his last world record race in 1931, when Lehtinen was leading him at 3,000 metres, but he came through in the last 200 yards to break 9 minutes for 2 miles.

Zatopek on this subject takes a different view. He believes in progress: just as the laser beam has followed the X-ray, Ron Clarke has displaced him. Although he agrees that George, Shrubb, Nurmi and himself could have run faster if set a higher target, they would still all have been beaten by Clarke, because he has developed his technique further, and is therefore the best possible runner to date. The argument is to some extent semantic, because the conditions can clearly never be reproduced, but Zatopek is not arguing in the Spinozan sense of the best of all possible worlds. His view is that science (or in this case running) is a continuous process, so that it is not possible to hark back from Einstein to Newton and claim that Newton might have discovered something which is an advance based on his own discoveries. This is a philosophically tenable view, and the two arguments show that the best long-distance runners apply a range of intelligence to their problems which is not matched by sportsmen in many other fields.

Leaving speculation aside, the next practical development after Zatopek had raised the sights was a spate of competitors of a higher standard than ever before. Two had already emerged and beaten Zatopek at 5,000 metres: Christopher Chataway and Vladimir Kuts. Chataway was the fastest of the distance runners. He did the crucial pacing at Oxford in May 1954, when Roger Bannister ran the mile inside 4 minutes for the first time ever. Chataway finished second in that race, and later on ran a mile in 3 mins 59.8 secs. If he had concentrated on the mile, he could undoubtedly have run it a good deal faster, but he chose the 3 miles and 5,000 metres as his speciality. His natural pace made him a dangerous man, as Kuts discovered on the unforgettable occasion in October 1954 in the match between London and Moscow at the White City.

This was a classic example of two completely different approaches to running, in which the more 'amateur' runner prevailed. Kuts was discovered in 1950 (as Zatopek said, rather in the way that America was discovered by Christopher Columbus). He seemed to be the first Soviet long-distance runner who could achieve world dominance,* and he was taken in hand by a team of experts who put him through a three years' course of scientific training. This was based partly on Zatopek's schedules of interval training, supplemented by muscle-building exercises, such as weight-lifting, gymnastics and jumping.

His schedule is opposite.

Thus, for three to four months of the year, Kuts was concentrating intensively on gymnastics, weight-lifting and jumping. Then for six to seven months he ran 10 kilometres a day fast. This was followed by two to three months on one of Zatopek's interval-training schedules: the 5/10/5, i.e. 5 times 200 metres plus 10 times 400 metres plus 5 times 200 metres, with jogging intervals of 200 metres. At the end of the year, he achieved 2 mins 45 secs for 1,000 metres.

In the second year he increased his strength-training by 100%,

---

* He was in fact the first Soviet athlete to win a gold medal in an Olympic track event.

stepped up his straight runs to between 15 to 20 kilometres, and increased his interval-training to 5/15/5, i.e. 5 times 200 plus 15 times 400 plus 5 times 200. In that year he was able to run 3,000 metres in 8 mins 25 secs.

In the third year he again did the double stint of strength-training, ran 20 kilometres a day straight, and increased his interval-training to 5/20/5. He achieved 14.01 mins for 5,000 metres, and was ready to be launched into international competition.

His first major race was against Zatopek in Bucharest in August of that year. In the 5,000 metres he led from the start and Zatopek caught him only in the last lap. In the 10,000 metres four days later, Zatopek won easily but Kuts, who finished second, had shown that he was potentially capable of beating Zatopek at the shorter distance.

At the end of the month, Kuts, Zatopek and Chataway met in the 5,000 metres race at the Berne European Games. Zatopek had already won the 10,000 metres. Kuts, who always ran from the front, went off at a great pace, and Chataway and Zatopek, who were more concerned with each other than with Kuts, let him open up too large a gap, and eventually had to fight each other for second place (which Chataway won) a good 100 metres behind Kuts.

Chataway's respect for Zatopek may have led him into a miscalculation on this occasion, but in the race in London two months later, he had only Kuts to consider.

Chataway was not a front runner. He is a professional man, well on his way to a political career which could take him any-where – perhaps even to Downing Street. There was no question of his spending three years being put through a full-time scientific system of training to make him the world champion. In his earlier days of competition, at Oxford, he limited his training to about half an hour on three or four days a week. Later, when he was seriously engaged in international athletics, he trained perhaps five times a week for an hour to an hour and a half. Therefore, he had to rely on his natural pace and his will-power to beat a man like Kuts, whose natural talent was boosted by a vast pro-gramme of full-time application to training.

The race at the White City on October 13th, 1954 was the most exciting in living memory because it was a contest between the brilliant professional (although not in the technical sense) and the brilliant amateur. Kuts went away from the start to build up a commanding lead (as at Berne) or to 'kill' Chataway if he should try to stay with him. Chataway refused to be 'killed' or left. The most exciting moment was at the three miles stage, where Kuts set a new record (13 mins 27 secs) with 188 yards to go, with Chataway running stride for stride behind him. Chataway has admitted that he was then so exhausted that he considered letting Kuts go, but in the last 60 yards he made a final effort of will, and his will-power and natural pace carried him past Kuts to win by about two yards in a new world record time of 13 mins 51.6 secs, for the 5,000 metres: the first time, incidentally, that an English runner had held a world record for a recognised metric distance.

Chataway did not hold this world record for long: the in-defatigable Kuts clipped $\frac{2}{5}$ second off it 10 days later in a race in Prague in which he also ran from the front and had no shadower. Chataway regained his 3 miles record the following year, but he was not interested in the full-time training schedules which were then necessary. He competed in the Melbourne Olympic Games at 5,000 metres, but dropped to 11th place because of an attack of stomach-cramp. At the Helsinki Games four years earlier, he was in with a chance in the last lap of the 5,000 metres, but stepped on the kerb of the track about 200 yards from the finish and fell. He got up, with typical courage, and still finished fifth. If he had not fallen, he would certainly have been second, and might even have won: but Zatopek was then finishing at a formidable speed, and it is doubtful whether even Chataway could have matched this.*

In 1955 and 1966 some new stars emerged. Sandor Iharos of Hungary set up a European record for 1,500 metres in 1954 and in 1955 broke the standard world records from 1,500 metres up to 5,000 metres. In 1956 he broke Zatopek's 6 miles and 10,000 metres records. He left Hungary after the suppression of the 1956 rising, and this was the end of his international career.

In the meantime, another British runner, Gordon Pirie, had been breaking records. He probably put in more work and time on training than any British runner since Shrubb, and in 1956 he beat Kuts in a 5,000 metres race in which he also beat Iharos's world record. Pirie, like Chataway, had great natural pace: he is the only one of the distinguished 10,000 metres runners who actually ran a mile in less than 4 minutes (Ron Clarke has done this, or its equivalent, but never for the record). Pirie's judgment was sometimes at fault. In 1956, in the weeks before the Melbourne Olympic Games, he took on a very strenuous programme of competition, in the course of which he set up a 3,000 metres world record, and then decided to contest both the 10,000 metres and 5,000 metres at Melbourne.

It is easy to be wise after the event, but it seems clear that if Pirie had not run in the 10,000 metres (which traditionally comes before the 5,000 in the Games) he might well have won the 5,000, for which he still held the world record. In the 10,000 metres race, Kuts employed his usual tactics of running the opposition into the ground, and succeeded, especially with Pirie, who courageously stayed with Kuts until the last mile, when he became exhausted and finished eighth. He had not recovered in the next 5 days sufficiently to challenge Kuts seriously in the shorter race, although he did finish second. Kuts won in 13 mins 39.6 secs, which was almost 3 seconds slower than Pirie's world record.

Pirie's performance in coming back, after his severe beating in the 10,000 metres, to finish second in the 5,000 deserves great credit. He ran for some years afterwards, but without any outstanding success.

At this time, the Hungarians had had a fairly brief ascendancy: Iharos, Tabori and Roszavolgyi were for a couple of years

* It is possible that fatigue was partly responsible for the fall.

remarkably difficult people to beat at anything from 1,500 metres to 10,000 metres.

Kuts ran his last great race in Rome in October 1957, when he lowered Pirie's world record for 5,000 metres by 1.8 seconds, to 13 mins 35 secs.

The effort seems to have overstrained him. He came off the track in a state of stupor and was taken away for treatment. Shortly afterwards he ran again at 10,000 metres and failed lamentably. Thereafter, an unspecified illness brought about his retirement. He was only 30 years old – 4 years younger than Nurmi when he set up his last world record – and he was a man of very strong physique. It is possible that his strictly controlled training schedule was too arduous for someone who did not participate, in the sense of working it out for himself, and willing it, as Zatopek did.

Certainly, Kuts did not dominate running in the way that George, Shrubb, Nurmi and Zatopek did. He won two gold medals at the 1956 Olympic Games, although if Iharos had been there and Pirie had stuck to the 5,000 metres, he might not have won either. But his career was shorter even than Chataway's, who was doing so much else besides running, and he was never the automatic winner of any race for which he was entered and fit, as Ron Clarke has been for the last three years. It is possible to argue that Soviet science may have overreached itself in the treatment of Kuts, and that, generally speaking, the top-class runners have to be people of marked intelligence as well as physical ability.

There was another very distinguished Soviet runner, Bolotnikov, who won the 10,000 metres race in the Rome Olympiad in 1960, and later set up a world record for the same distance of 28 mins 18.2 secs. But by then, although there were plenty of good European runners, the ascendancy had passed out of Europe, in fact down to the other side of the world.

Australian society is custom-made for high athletic standards. It is a vigorous, expanding society with plenty of space and opportunity for outdoor life. There is a high and widely diffused standard of living allowing time for leisure. Australian standards in other international sports like cricket and tennis are well-known, but it was not till about 1956 that running standards started to rocket. There was a similar activity in New Zealand, where conditions are comparable.

The trend was started by Albert Thomas, David Stephens and

Allan Lawrence. Thomas, who is only 5 ft. 5½ in. tall (1.65 m.) and weighed then 124 lb. (56 kg.) set up world 2 miles and 3 miles records in 1956, but finished only 5th at Melbourne. In 1958 he ran a mile in 3.56.8. Lawrence was 3rd in the 10,000 metres at Melbourne. Stephens put up a world 6 miles record earlier in the year but was not fit at the Olympics, and finished 20th. David Power was also in the top-class.

The trio of outstanding mile runners, Landy and Elliott of Australia, and Snell of New Zealand, did not compete at longer distances, but perhaps the most remarkable of all these athletes from Australasia was Murray Halberg of New Zealand, whose range was astonishing, as a look at his list of best performances shows:

800 metres	1 min. 51.7 secs
1,500 metres	3 mins 38.8 secs
1 mile	3 mins 57.5 secs
3,000 metres	7 mins 57.6 secs
2 miles	8 mins 30.0 secs
3 miles	13 mins 10.0 secs
5,000 metres	13 mins 52.2 secs
6 miles	27 mins 57.2 secs
10,000 metres	28 mins 48.0 secs
Marathon	2 hrs. 28 mins 43.0 secs

These peak performances were spread over a running career of nearly 7 years, from 1954 to 1961, during which Halberg broke the Olympic 5,000 metres record at Rome and was also 5th in the 10,000 metres. In 1961 he set up a new world record for 3 miles and failed by only two-fifths of a second to equal Kuts' 5,000 metres record. His 2 miles, 3 miles and 5,000 metres performances are still listed among the 10 best in the world respectively.

The most remarkable thing of all about him was that before his running career, he suffered a serious accident at Rugby Football which very nearly killed him and left him with a withered left arm, which ought to have upset the rhythm of his running and ruled him out of top-class competition. Apart from his immense courage and will-power, he demonstrated the contention of some coaches, notably Stampfl, that leg-action is the most important element in running, whatever the rest of the body is doing.

The long era of European ascendancy in distance running began to close after 1956, when Zatopek and Chataway were retiring,

Kuts had reached his zenith, the Hungarian school was in decline and British runners – although there were plenty of good ones – could not quite stay at the top. There was nothing sudden, like the overthrow of the Babylonian Empire, and there is no reason to believe it is permanent, but there was an unmistakable movement which might be called a Continental Drift. It became apparent at the Rome Olympic Games, where Snell and Elliott took the 800 and 1,500 metres races, Halberg the 5,000, and a man from yet another Continent, Abebe Bikila, ran away with the marathon. The only European in the distance races who asserted himself was Bolotnikov in the 10,000 metres; although the Polish runner, Krzyzkowiak won the 3,000 metres steeplechase, with Sokolov of the USSR 2nd.

At the Tokyo Olympic Games the drift was even more pronounced. Snell of New Zealand won the 800 metres and 1,500 metres. In the shorter race there was not a European in the first 6. In the 1,500 metres there were 3 (Odlozil of Czechoslovakia, Simpson of Britain and Baran of Poland) placed respectively 2nd, 4th and 6th. In the 5,000 metres, won by Schul of USA, Norpoth (Germany) and Jazy (France) in the 2nd and 4th places, were the only Europeans in the first 6. In the 10,000 metres Ivanov of Russia was 5th and after him the next European, Cervan of Yugoslavia, was 10th. In the Marathon, again won by Abebe, there were 4 Europeans in the first 10, including Heatley of Britain, who was 2nd.

The Continental Drift theory should not be exaggerated: European countries, including Britain, still have 'strength in depth', which is another way of saying that there is much more to the iceberg than the tip, and much of the underwater part is European. This means not only that there is a big body of European (including British) athletes just below the top level, but that the eight-ninths of the iceberg without which it could not float is analogous to the European development of distance running, and the European example and coaching, without which the other Continents would not have been able to achieve their present high placings.

Perhaps the best way to illustrate the Drift is by a comparative study of the World best performances in each year.* The picture

---

* Listed in *World Sports*, (annual) ed. Quercetani. This shows the gradual erosion of world records by new performances.

is somewhat confused by the metric and linear distances. British, American and Commonwealth runners compete more often at the mile, 3 miles and 6 miles; Continentals at the metric events. This is especially noticeable in the mile and 1,500 metres.

In 1963, for instance, the only Continental runner in the 13 best ever performances in the mile was the German, Valentin, in 7th place. In 10th and 11th places were the Englishman, Ibbotson, and the Irishman, Delany. Otherwise they were all New Zealanders, Australians or Americans, headed by Peter Snell, with Herbert Elliott 2nd. The 1,500 metres list for the same year is headed by Elliott, but 7 of the first 13 names are European. Michel Jazy, who does not appear in the mile list, is 2nd in the 1,500 metres, and Peter Snell is down to 9th. This does not necessarily represent the comparative merits of the athletes: it is simply that Jazy had not competed at a mile for some time, and Snell had not competed at 1,500 metres. He appeared at all in the 1,500 metres list because he happened to be timed *en route* in one of his mile races.

This factor is more significant in the 1,500 metres-mile comparison than in the longer races, but it still applies to them. In the 3 miles and 5,000 metres lists for the same year, 1963–4, Kuts and Bolotnikov do not appear in the 3 miles, because their best races at 5,000 metres had not been officially timed at the 3 miles mark. So only 2 Continentals, Iharos and Zimny, at 6 and 7, appear in this list. But at 5,000 metres Kuts is at the top and the balance favours the Europeans, of whom there are 8 (including Gordon Pirie) in the first 14. In the 10,000 metres, Ron Clarke was already at the top, but after him Europeans still predominated.

In the next year, 1964–5, the pendulum swung further. Ron Clarke now firmly headed both lists. Kuts and Bolotnikov were also both in the first half-dozen, but 7 of the first 14 names in the 5,000 metres list and 6 of the first 10 in the 10,000 metres are non-Europeans.

In the year 1965–66, there was a reshuffle in which Jazy, Herrmann, Michael Wiggs and Gaston Roelants all improved their performance at 5,000 metres and moved above Kuts, only to find another non-European, Keino of Kenya, who had also moved up, even above Ron Clarke, who was temporarily 2nd. In the 10,000 metres list, Clarke was still unshakeable, but there was a crop of fine performances in Europe: Roelants, Nikolay Dutov, Leonid

Ivanov and Lajos Mecser all improved their performances, but they could make no impression on Clarke, and the American, Mills, who had beaten them all at Tokyo, also improved.

The order was: Clarke, Roelants, Mills, Bolotnikov, Dutov, Gammoudi, which would have given the non-Europeans the edge in a team-race. In the next 8 placings, the Europeans predominated by 5 to 3.

If we come back to the question of depth – the tip of the iceberg and the rest – we can judge best not from the positions of the world record holder and his nearest pursuers, past and present, but from the list of the actual performances in order of merit in the last recorded year.

For 1966–67 there were 105 performances recorded at 5,000 metres of less than 14 mins 1 sec, each of which would have been a world record before May 30th, 1954. This in itself illustrates the upsurge in standards since Zatopek. It also illustrates the present supremacy of Ronald Clarke.

These are the 105 best performances, not the best 105 runners, because some athletes did more than one of the performances. The duplication is all in the top 32 performances, which were all within 13 mins 44 secs, and of these Ron Clarke did 11, (including the actual record, which was 8 seconds faster than anyone else could run). Tracy Smith, of the USA did 3, Keino, Gammoudi, Jazy and Makarov (USSR) did 2 each. This means that there are 16 names in the list of the 32 best performances of the year, and another 73 runners who each produced 1 performance inside 14 minutes.

Of the top 16, only 7 are Europeans, and their placings are: 2nd, 6th, 9th, 11th, 12th, 15th and 16th. The non-European nationalities are: Australian (2), Kenyan, Japanese, Tunisian, South African, American (3). If we count performances, not heads, the proportion in the top 32 is: Europe 8, the Rest 24.

If we, however, look further down the iceberg to the depth, we find it more in Europe, with 61 of the best 100 performances and 59 of the best 84 performers. The greatest depth in any one nation is in the Soviet Union, with 20 athletes in the first 100. 2nd comes the United States, with 8.

In a similar comparison of the 10,000 metres, Europe comes out better. Although there was only 1 European in the first 9 places at the Tokyo Olympics, 24 of the best 32 performances in

1966–67 were European. Ron Clarke was still out in front by 18.6 seconds over Jurgen Haase, of East Germany, who looked the most impressive European prospect for 1967 at that distance, and 3 Americans were well-placed.

Moreover, a glance at the 6 miles for that year shows that the 10,000 list is not representative. Naftali Temu of Kenya was 2nd to Ron Clarke in 6 miles performances, and his time was faster than the 10,000 metres equivalents of both Haase and Roelants, who were 2nd and 3rd at that distance. Gammoudi, also, was 3rd in the 6 miles list in a time worth 4th or 5th place in the 10,000 metres ratings. And 4 Americans who do not appear in the 10,000 metres list ran fast 6 miles races.

This alters the picture at the top, although the depth lies strongly with Europe, and particularly with Great Britain.

The challenge to Europe comes from all quarters of the globe. The excellence of Japanese and Australasian runners is now almost a tradition, but perhaps the most surprising new development is the resurgence of the Americans in distance-running. The Americans have always had a fine tradition of middle-distance running. They have won the Olympic 800 metres 7 times and the 1,500 metres 5 times. In earlier years they were prominent in the marathon: they took the first 3 places in 1904, 1st, 3rd and 4th in 1908 and 3rd and 4th in 1912. Since the First World War they have done very little at 1,500 metres or above, but they have remained consistently powerful at 800 metres until the last 2 Olympiads.

At Rome no United States citizen was in the first 6 – something unknown since the 1st Olympiad of 1896, when the Americans were sparsely represented, although an American (C. J. Kilpatrick) held the world record at the time. At Tokyo, where Snell of New Zealand won both 800 metres and 1,500 metres, the Americans, Farrell and Siebert, finished 5th and 6th in the shorter event and Burleson 5th in the longer. (This state of affairs was transitory: the 800 metres and the mile world records are now held by the American, Jim Ryun, with 5 other Americans listed in the best 10 performances at the $\frac{1}{2}$-mile, and 3 at the mile.)

What was more significant at Tokyo was that Americans for the first time won the distance races. Their best previous effort had been 2nd in the 10,000 metres in 1912 and 2nd in the 5,000 in 1932. The interest – and excellence – in the longer track races is a wholly new departure. American athletics has traditionally followed a marked racial pattern. In the 'explosive' events requiring great speed and power, American Negroes have established the ascendancy over their white compatriots: that is, in the sprints and long-jump, now extending to the 400 metres. In the explosive events requiring greater technique than speed, e.g. throwing events, hurdling, pole-vault, the white (or Caucasian) Americans have been supreme, and can be matched only by the Russians. Negroes have had some success in the high-jump and hurdles events, but by and large their ascendancy is in the events requiring explosive speed, not endurance, and they seldom race more than 800 metres, if that.

The Americans of European origin have shown the ability and inclination to pursue the whole range of athletic competition. They live in a highly competitive society, with a powerful technological base, so it is not surprising that when they apply themselves to the techniques of field events they should be outstandingly successful, or that they should develop so many outstanding middle-distance runners. What is surprising is that there should have been so little activity in longer-distance running in the past half-century, either by coloured or white Americans.

The period coincides with the mass motorisation of American life. Americans are notoriously reluctant to use any form of loco-motion except the automobile. They even shop and cash cheques without getting out of their cars, and use stairs only for film-sets. This has sometimes been advanced as a reason for the lack of interest in distance-running. But the preparation required for, say, a pole-vault competition, and the exertion of 10 concentrated vaults spread over 2 hours or more in a competition is as arduous as a 5,000 metre schedule. Again, the accelerator pedal can give a sense of power which may substitute for the athletic impulse, but only to a fairly low form of mentality, and this is certainly not found in American athletes of any sort. Most of them are students and they obviously bring a high mental capacity to their mastery of athletic techniques.

A more plausible explanation lies in the absence of a tradition of cross-country running, such as Britain has maintained, and the high degree of urbanisation even in the less populated areas. There is also the influence of national tradition. The Finnish school of distance runners had a strong influence on other Continental countries – Germany, Sweden, Czechoslovakia, Poland, Hungary and finally Russia. Looking back, there is a historical pattern of European schools of running as of painting, which flourished for a period and passed on their influence to other countries. This process took a long time to cross the Atlantic, but now that it has, we may expect to see performances like those of Schul, Dellinger, Mills and Edelen at Tokyo maintained and improved on.

As regards the coloured American athletes, there may be an explanation of their performance in inherited physique. It is scarcely necessary to travel in Africa to observe that there is no African type. Africa is a Continent in which, owing to the persistence of a traditional economy, there has been much less miscegenation than in Europe, and the physical characteristics of tribal groups are more clearly preserved. The subject of racial characteristics is dangerous ground: more nonsense has been talked and written about them, from Gobineau and Houston Chamberlain onwards, than about anything else. But some physical characteristics are recognisable in areas where for some reason they have been isolated. This happened to some extent with American Negroes, who represent largely a slice of Western Africa transshipped in the nefarious slave trade to America and then preserved for many generations owing to racial prejudice which limited miscegenation.

A physical type frequently found among American Negroes is powerfully built but also long-limbed and remarkably fluent in movement. This type provides perfect material for sprinting and long-jumping. Jesse Owens was the greatest of all. It also provides the material for the very highest class of heavy-weight boxer. Cassius Clay (or Mohammed Ali) has incredible speed of movement for a man of his weight, and this has made him probably the best boxer in modern times (together with his concentration: in spite of his deliberate fooling for publicity purposes he always carries out a training schedule comparable in its way with Zatopek's).

This physical type, with greater variations, is also found among the West Indians, who have an immense talent for sporting activities. In athletics this has been largely confined to the shorter distances, and came out strongly in the 400 metres. In 1952 the small island of Jamaica beat the United States by 1 yard in the 4 × 400 metres relay, to set up a new Olympic and world record at Helsinki, both of which records stood for 8 years. At Tokyo, the United States won the 4 × 400 metres relay, and Britain was 2nd. 3rd and 4th were the islands of Trinidad and Jamaica, in front of the Great Powers: Germany, Poland, the Soviet Union and France.

There is another African physical type which has a different potential and has already shown it. Any visitor to Eastern Africa with a nose for athletic potential will see tall, willowy types with long limbs and flat muscles. They are Nilotic or Nilo-Hamitic and abound in Abyssinia, South Sudan, Uganda and Kenya. They have already been seen in action in world class athletics: Abebe Bikila of Ethiopia won the Rome Olympic Marathon in 2 hrs 15 mins 16.2 secs, and came back at Tokyo 4 years later to win again in 2 hrs 12 mins 11.2 secs. Another Ethiopian, Mamo Wolde, was 4th in the 10,000 metres, just behind Ron Clarke. Kipchoge Keino of Kenya was 5th in the 5,000 metres. Since then, Keino has improved his 5,000 metres performance to 13 mins 24.2 secs, 2nd only to Ron Clarke. Naftali Temu, also of Kenya, has run the 4th fastest 6 miles. Keino has also come very close to the 1,500 metres and mile records, and another Kenyan, Benjamin Kogo, ran the fastest 3,000 metres steeplechase in 1967.

These are all portents of the great potential of Eastern Africa, which has only begun to develop. There is no parallel with Australia, where a generally high standard of living encourages sporting activities. What the East Africans seem to have is an immense reservoir of natural talent and wherever modern methods of training can be applied, as the Kenyans are increasingly doing, the results are bound to be outstanding. There is also a great potential in that part of the world for high-jumping. There are people there who, given the coaching and facilities that Brumel, Thomas and others have had in the United States and the Soviet Union, are capable of clearing over 7 ft. 6 in. (2.30 metres).

The facilities to tap this great potential fully do not yet exist, but the new school of Kenyan runners has made a brilliant start. There is the further advantage both in Kenya and Ethiopia that athletes can train at high altitudes.

The decision to stage the XIX Olympic Games in Mexico City, at 7,400 ft. above sea level, has aroused great controversy mainly

Above: Gundar Haegg in 1945: the world's best at One to Three Miles.
Below: One of the great Hungarians: L. Tabori, 5,000 metres, 1960. Tulloh
was second

Zatopek comes in from the Marathon for his third Olympic Gold Medal,
Helsinki 1952

on two grounds: first that there could be medical danger to athletes unaccustomed to the altitude, and secondly that there is an unfair advantage to athletes who have an opportunity of training at the altitude. There does not seem to be any medical evidence to support the first contention. A medical research project was carried out in Mexico City in 1965 by a physiological team under Dr L. G. C. Pugh and Dr Raymond Owen, the Honorary Medical Officer to the British Olympic Association. The effects of high-altitude performance were studied exhaustively and no evidence was found of any danger to the health of the competitors. The team did note in its report that officials who had any cardiac weakness or suffered from any respiratory complaint might be in danger, but this would obviously not apply to any athlete considered medically fit for Olympic competition.

The second point has more substance and raises acutely the principle of amateur status and the rules of fair competition. A third point which has received less attention is perhaps more important in the long term. The focusing of attention on the altitude problem at Mexico City has led to more intensive study of the actual influence of altitude on performance. It was already well-known that a rapid rise in altitude impairs performance in endurance events by restricting oxygen-intake. What has also emerged is that an athlete, once acclimatised to the higher altitude, not only suffers no disadvantage in going down to perform at sea-level, but actually is at an advantage over an opponent who has trained only at sea-level.

Various countries which can afford it, and possess the necessary mountains, have set up full-scale training camps at about the same height as Mexico City – the Americans in Colorado and the Russians in the Caucasus. Not much has been heard about the Soviet experiment, but American athletes have found that after a spell of high-altitude training their performance at ground-level has improved over 1 and 3 miles.

This discovery introduces a new element into training potentially as important as the development of interval-training. Ron Clarke suggested in London recently that if international competitions are to be held at altitudes like that of Mexico City, there may have to be a grading of records according to height from sea-level, just as with aircraft, mach (the speed of sound) varies with altitude. This is a practical suggestion, but it does not meet the

H

difficulty of assessing the advantage enjoyed by athletes able to train at high altitude.

On the other hand, it is unlikely that the Olympic Games will again be held at the Mexico City altitude as far ahead as can be seen, since virtually all the countries able to provide facilities for the monumental requirements of an Olympiad in fact have their capital cities at or near sea-level.

In the meantime, Ron Clarke is firmly established as the world champion distance-runner, still well out in front. When the challenge to his records comes, we may expect it from one of the countries with full-scale facilities for altitude-training: Kenya, Abyssinia, the USA, France, Germany or the USSR.

8
Why Do They Run?

The essence of athletics is competition. It should be a balance between man against man and man against nature, that is, the result of the race and the standard of performance as compared with all other comparable recorded performances. This balance is generally maintained. The spectators at a meeting usually have their enthusiasm kindled first by the struggle on the track between man and man, especially if it is a close one. The second element – the record – gives an added piquancy. The viewers are participating in an historic occasion, when they learn that they have witnessed somebody doing something better than it has ever been done before.

In the most exciting of competitions, the Olympic Games, it has been rare for the winners to break world records, and the main attention is on man against man, with an additional element of partisanship owing to nationalist feelings. This intrusion of national prestige into Olympic competition is not in keeping with the Olympic ideal of Baron Couvertin and the other founders of the modern Games, which were to have been truly international, not inter-national. But it would have been naïve in the extreme to expect anything else, and it is remarkable how little friction has been engendered at the Games by nationalist fervour. What remains behind in world consciousness after an Olympiad is not quotas of gold, silver and bronze won by this nation or that, but the splendid individual performances of Nurmi, Lovelock, Jesse Owens, Zatopek, Elliott or Abebe.

In writing and commentary about athletics, there is a tendency to concentrate too much on the aspect of man against nature – the recorded performances. A good deal of technical writing on athletics also tends to be esoteric because it is mainly the work of

115

coaches and other experts trying, rightly, to explain to younger athletes how to improve their performances. There is a danger that the emphasis on statistics may dehumanise athletics. This computer approach overlooks the personality and individualism which is the basis and the heart of athletic competition.

There is a theory that if an athlete of any promise is prepared to put himself body and soul into the hands of a really scientific coach for a period of years, he can be processed into a champion by interval-training, weight-lifting, diet, technical advice, and so on, and especially psychological influence. This does not correspond with a study of the personalities of most of the really great distance-runners. There has been since 1880 a series of athletes who each for a period reigned supreme at distances upwards of a mile: W. G. George, Alfred Shrubb, Paavo Nurmi, Emil Zatopek, Vladimir Kuts, Ronald Clarke. There were many others over the period who broke records or won Olympic medals, but there was about all these an aura of quality which enabled them to dominate the athletic scene.

Walter Goodall George was born in Calne, Wiltshire, in 1858. He came of middle-class parents with a farming background. He competed in local sports-meetings at first, at distances from 100 yards to a mile, and ran cross-country. By the time he was 21, that is, 1879, the split between the Amateur Athletic Club and the regions occurred and 2 rival championships were held. At one of these, he won the mile and the 4 miles, and in the following year, at the inaugural AAA Championships, he also won the mile and 4 miles. He did not compete in 1881 and 1883, but in each of the years 1882 and 1884 he won the $\frac{1}{2}$-mile, mile, 4 miles and 10 miles.

His mile time in 1884 was 4 mins 18$\frac{2}{5}$ secs, which remained the world amateur record until 1893. In 1884 a Scottish professional, William Cummings, was reported to have run a mile in 4 mins 16$\frac{1}{5}$ secs, and George asked for permission to run against him as an amateur. His proposal was that Cummings should receive half the gate money, and the other half should be given to a hospital. Unfortunately, this was a time when amateurism was a very hot potato. A campaign was still going on to stop professionals from running under assumed names in amateur meetings where saleable objects like silverware were awarded as prizes, and the authorities could not make an exception, in any circumstances, to the rules which they were struggling so hard to enforce. George should have realised this – as in later years he did – but he could not resist the challenge of a better performance. He therefore gave up his amateur status, and ran against Cummings in 1885, setting up his world record of 4 mins 12¾ secs.

This incident is characteristic of George. Off the track, he was a kindly, mild-mannered man, and did not exploit his professional status. Nor was he obsessed with statistics. But on the track he went out to win – and always did when he was fit. What he could not tolerate was a notionally better performance which he was not allowed to challenge. There was no amateur miler who could extend George at the time. In the event, he ran Cummings into the ground.*

Like most of his successors, the really great runners, George possessed more than great natural ability – although he had plenty of that. He had also considerable intelligence and great will-power. His training schedules were much less arduous and systematic than they would have to be now, but he did a good deal of work and put an edge on his performance by constant competition. He normally ran 2 races on a Saturday in summer – a ½-mile and a mile – and sometimes a 3rd. At the AAA meeting on Saturday 21st June 1884 he won the ½-mile, mile and 4 miles championships and on the 2nd day of the meeting, Monday 23rd, he took the 10 miles in 54.02 which, like his mile on the Saturday, was a Championship record. (A few weeks later, he reduced his 10 miles time to 51 mins 20 secs, and this stood as a world record for 20 years.) During the winter, George used to do strenuous cross-country running, and was twice National Champion.

He was temperamentally a front runner, and could not often find anyone to press him, but he was also a good tactical runner with a fast finish when necessary.

George had a fine physique: 5 ft. 11 in. (1.80 metres) weighing about 10½ stones (147 lb.) at his peak of condition. Even when I first met him in his early fifties, he had the unmistakable cut of the athlete, and 20 years later he could still be seen at most track-meetings in South London, a slim, upright figure, always wearing a gold AAA Championship medal, in the Edwardian fashion, on his watch-chain.

When George reached his 70th birthday, in 1928, he was enter-

* See page 119.

tained as the honoured guest of the National Sporting Club, which even to this day has something of the Victorian atmosphere of patronage of professionals by gentlemen. George had once upon a time been a professional, but he was also always a gentleman. Sir Charles Allom, one of the patrons, spoke of George's 'ceaseless and invaluable efforts to teach the younger generation not only the true art of running but the true meaning and spirit of sportsmanship'. This meant that George had put in a good deal of time between 1918 and 1928 in coaching and encouraging young runners, and his aberration in declaring himself a professional 43 years before had been condoned by the Establishment.

When W. G. George died in 1943, one of the obituaries written about him was by Joe Binks, a very fine runner who knew George well and beat his amateur mile record, (although not his 'professional' one) and afterwards did a great deal to encourage athletics when he became the Athletics Editor of the *News of the World*, which, on his advice, began the practice in England of sponsoring athletics meetings, to which leading athletes from other countries were invited to compete. These meetings, called the 'British Games', have been held annually since 1923.

Joe Binks wrote in his obituary notice in the *News of the World* of 6th June 1943 that George never trained seriously, except for his mile race against Cummings in 1886. So, he wrote, 'one will never know how good he was when he really meant business'. With all respect to the late Joe Binks, to whom many athletes owe a very great debt, he may have taken George's protestations too seriously. After a season out of amateur athletic competition, George obviously had to put in more individual training than he had been used to, and he did at that time pay more attention to lap-timings than he had previously done. Joe Binks went on:

'Walter [George] won 12 AAA track championships (880 yards, 1, 4 and 10 miles) and set up records from 1,000 yards to the hour. He won the Northern 2 miles title, and over country twice won the Midland and National championships.

'He told me that Billy Snook* was his greatest opponent and that he worried the life out of him in scores of races.

---

* W. Snook, of Birchfield Harriers, won the AAA mile, 4 miles and 10 miles in 1883 and 1885, and the Cross-country championship in 1885. George did not compete as an amateur after 1884.

'In 1884 Walter had a remarkable year and was just unbeatable at anything in running. In the Easter week, for instance, he won the LAC London 10 miles in record time (51 mins 26⅔ secs) and the 880 yards, mile and mile steeplechase at the West of Scotland meeting.

'He then travelled back to Woodbridge, Suffolk, to win the 880 yards, mile and 2 miles steeplechase handicap. I could quote a score of similar outstanding successes.

'The reason Walter came to run Cummings for the professional championship is interesting. He wanted to prove to the world that he could beat anybody, but as he wished to remain an AAA amateur, he asked for permission to run Cummings "for a gold medal or nothing", and that his share of the gate money should go to charity.

'That suggestion horrified the AAA, and they would not allow it. George, however, determined that he would prove himself the best in the world, and fixed up with Cummings.

'And what a race! Before 25,000 excited people, George was off first and led around the first lap by ¾ of a yard, in 58½ secs. Cummings quickened up, but George lengthened his stride and held the lead at 880 yards in 2 mins 1¾ secs. People were yelling with excitement at the fast time.

'Approaching the ¾-mile mark, Cummings drew up again, but George would not let him get to the front. So they raced stride for stride, and the bookmakers yelled "100 to 1 on Cummings!" '

'Around that furious last lap, especially when passing the stands, Cummings just led for the first time. Along the back straight, however, George drew level again, and by now everybody knew they were watching racing such as never was seen before.

'George sprinted at the hospital end of the track, but Cummings responded and looked to be the winner, only waiting for the final burst.

'As they came into the straight, with George just ahead, Cummings made another desperate challenge.

'George put in his final effort about 60 yards from home, when the gallant Cummings cracked and fell exhausted, leaving George to finish alone in the then astounding time of 4 mins 12¾ secs.'

At that time there was a great flurry about training diet. It has for long been realised that the Victorian and post-Victorian idea

of what athletes should eat or avoid eating was not very scientific.
It consisted in eating a lot of protein, drinking very little liquid
and taking purgatives because the lack of liquid tended to con-
stipation. George, who had lived through all this theory, said 'My
favourite training diet was a glass of beer with some bread and
cheese'.

The next in succession after George was Alfred Shrubb. He was
a small man and on the surface un-athletic-looking. He had small
bones and flat muscles. Stripped down (to the extent that anyone
was then allowed to strip down into sleeved vests and long shorts)
he looked very different. He was certainly not one of the great
brains of his generation, as he showed when he went into print
in 1910 with a book called *Running and Cross-country Running,
by Alfred Shrubb* (The World's Greatest Pedestrian).

This is a very bad book, which suggests that Shrubb was un-
intelligent. When he tries to sell his views on diet and training
against those of other experts, he says: 'Although my experience
may not have been so *lengthy* as those of others, I have reason
to believe it to be quite as *extensive,* seeing that I have run more
long-distance races in the past 2 years than others have in 5.' He
goes on to refer to the 'measure of success' which has 'fallen to
him', which is a rather pompous way of saying that he thinks
very highly of his own performance. He was also very patriotic,
and thought that, in spite of the recent successes of the Americans
in international competition, 'the doggedness of the Briton should
prevail'.

This, and most of what Shrubb put on paper, sounds rather
stupid, when it is not pompous. Yet when Shrubb gets down to
explaining his training schedules, he makes a great deal of sense.*
So do his ideas about diet. They were the first systematic
training schedules for long-distance running in modern times.
If the ancient Greeks had any, they have not been recorded.
Shrubb may have been the origin of the widely-held belief that
long-distance runners are introvert. But, apart from him, only
Nurmi among the great ones dealt with in this chapter could be
called introvert. George, Zatopek, Chataway and Clarke were certainly not.

Shrubb could not communicate. In my own experience, in the
2 years in which I was a member of the Oxford University

* Chapter IV.

Athletic Club – while he was coach, he addressed me only once, and his advice was not to run on the inside of the track, because it had been raining and he did not want it to be damaged. This was sensible enough: although there was a groundsman whose job it was to look after the track, and Shrubb's job was to spot and encourage talent. I turned out afterwards, according to performance, to have been the best potential at his own distances that he then had, but it was his successor, Thomas, and outsiders like Joe Binks and Harry Payne, who gave me advice and encouragement.

Nevertheless, Shrubb's intelligence should not be underrated because he did irresponsible things when he was a professional, and wrote a rather stupid book. After all, Cerutty has written a book with which many thoroughly disagree, yet he has a shrewd intelligence about physical training, and certainly helped several top-class Australian athletes to get to the top. In the same way, Shrubb talks sense when he gets on to practical matters. He was probably much more intelligent than the image of himself which he presented.

Shrubb's achievement was impressive. Although he lacked the pace of George, Nurmi and Chataway, who could all put on at least a respectable $\frac{1}{2}$-mile, as well as a very fast mile, he did evolve a system of training for distances from 3 miles to 10 miles which to some extent foreshadowed that of Nurmi, and some of his records stood for 20 years or more.

After Shrubb, the next great figure was Nurmi, who had much more in common with George. He had George's combination of pace and stamina, and could also compete at the top-level from 800 metres upwards. He also had the benefit of the Finnish tradition of distance running. Nurmi, like George, was reserved. He disliked publicity and fanfares, and tried to keep out of their way. He was also, like George, a modest and kindly man. He could snub a photographer or autograph-hunter, but even that he did gently, and he could be kind and encouraging to a young athlete and always scrupulously polite to his opponents, whether they lost or (very rarely) won.

Nurmi's methods and achievements have also been dealt with in detail. What we are concerned with here is his character and his attitude to running. He was patriotic. Finland was a newly independent republic but an old civilisation with a strong national and cultural consciousness when Nurmi's international career began. He, more than anyone else, put Finland on the map. In the century before 1914 Finland had passed from being a Swedish protectorate to a Russian protectorate, although it had retained its identity. After 1918 it became a nation in its own right, and has remained so. Nurmi, although he does not talk much about it, is well aware of his contribution to this. As, later, with Zatopek, it added a dimension to his motive in athletics. He was also influenced by the very cultivated pursuit of athletic excellence which centred in the Kohlemainen family and their friends.

Over and above this, Nurmi was the greatest runner up to his time and, although he was always embarrassed to say so, must have been aware of it. He was a perfectionist and a scientist in running. He brought even-paced running to near perfection and was more conscious of the stop-watch than any runner before him, not because he cared too much for records or statistics, but because pacing – or the stop-watch – was his instrument for achieving his ideal, which was simply to win every race in the best time in which it could be run by current standards.

This required (over and above the natural ability) an immense volume of hard work in training, intelligence applied to both training and tactical running, and the immense will to win. Like most of the other great athletes, Nurmi was ruthless on the track, and magnanimous off it. He also had remarkable self-control. When I first met him, just before a race in which I was also running, he was asleep on a trestle-table, with a blanket round him. He was able to go to sleep for half an hour before a race, when everyone else was using up nervous energy by feeling plumb scared. He got up, yawning but polite, shook hands and said a few kindly words, went out on the track to warm up, went to his marks, and knocked nearly half a minute off a world record. In the shower-baths afterwards, when congratulated, he was deprecatory and said: 'Not a good time; the track was bad'. This was quite true. The track was in very bad condition and Nurmi finished half a minute outside the schedule which he had planned on the assumption of a reasonable surface, which would have given him 29 minutes for 6 miles.

Paavo Nurmi was in one sense the gentlest of the great runners. Most of them, on the track, direct their ruthlessness – their need to win – against their opponents. For the brief period of the competition, they can even hate the adversary, although they will be the first to shake hands with him once the tape – and tension – is broken. Nurmi was more detached from his adversaries than any of the others, because he ran against a planned schedule which he had to beat. Only when personal opponents threatened to beat the schedule too, did he have to throw in all he had against the man, instead of the schedule. But he did not need to feel strongly about his opponent to do this. He simply forgot his schedule and went hell-for-leather towards the end, and it almost always worked.

This detachment, together with Nurmi's naturally retiring temperament, has fostered the idea that he was unapproachable, but this is not true. He would, by contemporary standards, be a bad soccer star, who has to be hugged and kissed, and then patted on the back by teenagers, when he has scored a goal. But his dislike of demonstrativeness was not due to any lack of human sympathy. Nowadays in Helsinki, as a successful businessman, he no doubt still dislikes back-slappers and autograph-hunters, but he is always kind and hospitable to people with a genuine interest in athletics who call on him.

There was a certain rough chronology about the emergence of very great runners: W. G. George was at his peak in 1884, Shrubb in 1904, Nurmi about 1924. Zatopek took a little longer to emerge. His first international impact was in 1946, but there had been the most total of wars raging from 1939 to 1945. There had been Wooderson and Haegg in between, but since Zatopek the gap has narrowed. Kuts overran him, although he had not the same scope, and did not last as long.

The importance of Zatopek has already been discussed. Although he was unbeatable at 3 miles and 5,000 metres until those 2 formidable adversaries, Kuts and Chataway, caught up with him, he was really better at the longer distances. In a recent letter (which I have quoted above*) he said: 'I was really better at 10,000 metres than 5,000 metres. In 1951, I was especially proud of my 20,000 metres record (59 mins 21.2 secs) and 1 hour race (20,052 metres).' He added, incidentally: 'My only 2 marathons were in Helsinki and Melbourne Olympics.'

This is a remarkable tribute to his training methods. In each case he was competing with the world's best. The first time he

* Chapter 5.

won. The second time, as he puts it: 'Later I was worse and worse (tired) and in Melbourne Olympics 1956 – after my hernia operation – I was able to run only marathon (6th place).'

Most athletes (with or without a hernia operation) who had got a place in the first 6 in an Olympic event in recent years would still be dining out on it. Zatopek records it almost apologetically.

Just as he narrowly missed a world record with his second run over the full 10,000 metres distance, and won an Olympic Gold Medal with his third, he moved straight to the top in his marathon appearances. His 20,000 metres and 1 hour records were his first systematic attempts at those distances.

This speaks volumes for his system of training. It also reveals a great deal about his character and the intelligence he brought to his running.

Zatopek worked out his own methods, as we have seen. He is much more extrovert than Nurmi, and more willing to talk: he is in fact a most stimulating and amusing conversationalist. He took up competitive running for the simple reason that he found he was good at it, and, having taken it up, worked out his own pro-gramme for doing it better than anyone else. Like George and Nurmi, he always went out to win, and if there was a record he wanted to break it. Talking to Zatopek, one finds that he has a hair-trigger memory of his athletic career. He can remember every race in detail – where he felt bad, where he piled on the pressure, where he made a tactical error, when his training brought him a world record. This is simply an aspect of his power of concentration.

In his training he punished himself until fatigue scarcely meant anything to him. On the track he had only one idea: to beat the opposition. His methods and technique have already been dis-cussed. Here we are concerned with his personality as an athlete and a man. Like George and Nurmi, he was disinterested. It is not possible to be the best runner in the world without deriving some fringe-benefits from it, and some athletes have certainly had that in mind. Zatopek entered the Czech Army before the begin-ning of his international career, and his success probably helped him in his Army career. About the time he won the Olympic 10,000 metres in London in 1948, he was promoted from 2nd Lt. to 1st Lt., and the editor of a Czech paper attacked this pro-motion as a form of professionalism, or 'shamateurism'. Zatopek was hurt – it is one of the few things on which he still speaks with some sense of grievance. At about the same time, he married his wife, Dana, who had also competed at the 1948 Olympic Games, and won the Women's Javelin at Helsinki in 1952.

Zatopek's view was that he, as a serving officer, now had to support a wife, on a slightly increased salary, who was free to train for her own international competition. Why should he be accused of professionalism, when he was on balance rather worse off?

Perhaps a stronger argument would have been that he was a very efficient officer, and would have got promotion anyway, but Zatopek was too modest to use this argument, and too logical. His answer to his detractor put a finger on the whole illogicality of the theory of amateurism, and this is typical of Zatopek's well-organised mind. He goes to the nub of the matter.

Zatopek's army career has been a successful one, not because of his athletic honours, but because of his qualities of mind and character, which would have made a mark in any profession. Obviously, a military career, with its background of physical fitness, suited an athlete, and, like an athletic soldier in any other army, he could often get a dispensation to train while others were doing routine PT or square-bashing. But this gave him no more than the advantage enjoyed by a student or a teacher of Physical Education. There is no evidence that his promotion was due to his athletic distinction. He became a Colonel after the normal span of service, and his post in the Ministry of Defence, organising sport in the Army, is an obvious appointment and an important one in a peace-time army.

As we have seen, Zatopek thought deeply about athletic training and competition. In general he is not ambitious and is well satisfied with the position his 23 years in the army have brought him. But on the running-track he was perhaps the most aggressive of all runners. He once remarked that the text 'Blessed are the poor in spirit' may be good ethics, but it does not apply to competitive running, where he was always actuated by a 'primitive desire to win'. His training created the machine capable of winning, but he believes very strongly that the ultimate factor is in the mind and heart – the 'moral plus'. Just as he does not apply the Sermon on the Mount to competition, he equally rejects materialism. In his training and racing he applied what he called the 'optimal function': the combination of the trained physique with the intense mental and psychological effort required to pull out the last reserves.

On one occasion, when he was discussing the use of drugs, Zatopek said that he had once experimented with a drug which he had previously used before and during examinations to aid concentration, but in running it was less than useless: his performance over 1,500 metres was 2 seconds slower than without the drug (some sort of benzedrine). He had qualified as a pharmacist just before then.

His view now is that drugs cannot increase performance (although in very extended efforts like 6-day bicycle races they may enable a competitor to keep going a bit longer). Zatopek says that the only drugs that are any use to an athlete in his line of business are those he creates himself. He meant metabolism, such as the discharge from adrenal and other glands controlled by emotional conditions. This, he believes, is part of the control of mind over matter which adds the last, imponderable element to the physical performance. The fright before the start, when the adrenal is building up, is the outward sign. It used to be called wind-up, the first syllable referring to the element which bloweth where it listeth, but it could equally be pronounced as what is done by winches or clockwork. It serves both functions.

What Zatopek believes is expressed in the word psychosomatic, which simply means the influence of the mind on the body, although generally used in the morbid sense of the mind imposing diseases on the body. There is no reason why it should be.

The great physician, Galen (Claudius Galenus) who lived in the 2nd Century AD, and had certainly a longer influence on medicine than anyone else (it extended for over 1,000 years) in one of his many treatises dealing with physical fitness, called the *Treatise on the Small Ball*, wrote: 'Of all the affections that are rooted in the body, none is strong enough to master those that have the mind for their sphere. So it is wrong to neglect the character of our mental emotions.' If Zatopek had been born about 1,800 years before he actually was, he might have expressed himself in those terms. But he would not have seen eye-to-eye with Galen, who thought ball-games superior to athletics. If Galen had been contemporary with Zatopek, he might have spent more of his time at Lords than at the White City, but either way there would have been a basis of agreement on the relation between mind and body.

Zatopek has fully described his own training methods, but he does not believe that it is any use merely following someone else's schedule. The essence of his method was the application of 'creative intensity' to training, and his methods were no more than a sign that it is possible to increase ability by intensive work. He also believes that it is not possible to reach the top without intelligence. It is not merely that a race at the top level is a battle of wits and judgment under conditions of great stress. It is rather that Zatopek believes no one can create his own training system and apply it to the best advantage unless he is intelligent.

This implies that it is necessary to be an individualist to get to the top, and the man who has to follow blindly the instructions of a coach in the whole of his training will not be enough of an individualist to beat other strong individuals. Similarly, if he goes it alone he must be intelligent enough to find his own system.

Towards the end of his career, Zatopek was caught up by two other distinguished athletes, Chataway and Kuts. He might reasonably have hoped to finish his career by winning the Olympic marathon at Melbourne in 1956 before retiring, but he had to undergo his hernia operation in 1956 which ruled this out. He took it easy, by his standards, and finished 6th in a race won by the French-Algerian, Alain Mimoun Okacha, who had finished 2nd to Zatopek in 5 major races. It was almost the only race in which Zatopek was tolerant to his adversaries and merely aimed at finishing in a respectable position. Having aimed at no more than that, he was quite glad that Mimoun had at last won a major honour.

Not much is known about Kuts. He was 'discovered' in 1952 and taken in hand by a team of trainers and scientists, who built him up into a world champion. His period of ascendancy was short, and his finest hour was in the Melbourne Olympic Games, when he won the 5,000 and 10,000 metres races. Until then, Chataway had slightly the edge on him at 5,000 metres, and Zatopek at 10,000. He was a fine natural athlete who might have done even better if he had been allowed, and encouraged, to work out his own destiny.

Christopher Chataway, who was neck and neck with Kuts at the end of Zatopek's career, was a distinctively English phenomenon. He had the advantage of good training facilities at Oxford, and was contemporary with two other outstanding athletes, Bannister, who broke the 4-minute barrier for the mile, and Brasher, who won the Olympic 3,000 metres steeplechase at Melbourne. But when he left Oxford, he had only a limited period of top-class athletics, and even that was not full-time, because he had to prepare for a career elsewhere which could not be deferred very long.

Chataway ran because he knew he was good at running, and anyone, unless he is very odd, will want to do the thing at which he excels. He has distinguished between different levels of competition. In an essay in a book by the Achilles Club (which represents past and present athletes of the two older English Universities)* he said that an athlete nowadays has two courses open to him: 1) to settle for club competition, which will be enjoyable and unexacting, but will not bring in the sort of renown which enabled Greek Olympic champions to dine in the Town Hall for the rest of their lives, or 2) to venture into the hard wilderness of top-class competition, which will really be a full-time job as long as you are doing it.

He himself found some sort of compromise. He put a great deal of time and effort into training, but by restricting his appearances at the top-level, he managed to lay the foundations of a career, elsewhere. His compromise meant that in the world contests he could not quite keep up with the full-timers. At Melbourne in 1956, in the 5,000 metres, he had a stomach-cramp. In 1952 at Helsinki, he had been hot on the heels of Zatopek in the last lap, but had fallen through running too close and stepping on the board marking the margin of the track. Chataway scrambled up and finished 5th. Pirie wanted to tie with Chataway, but was judged 4th in the same recorded time as Chataway – 14 mins 18 secs. Ties are not recognised in Olympic competition.

Chataway was not worried about being placed 5th instead of equal fourth. He was more concerned about having tripped himself out of the race when he was about to challenge Zatopek over the last $\frac{1}{2}$-lap. He was a very fast finisher, capable of faster times than Zatopek at anything from 1 mile downwards.

* *Athletics*, ed. A. H. Meyer.

Left: Pirie, Zatopek and Norris in a fighting finish

Below: The hinterland of Portsea: Percy Cerutty, Elliott, Rimmer and Beck doing 'Fartlek'-style training

Herb Elliott winning at Cambridge: half-mile 1961

Christopher Chataway is the last of the real amateurs. For a couple of years he devoted a great deal of his time to athletics, but he was never subsidised – except perhaps by his parents. If he had had to choose between athletics and giving up his career outside athletics, he would certainly not have hesitated to make the longer term choice. He went into politics and was one of the able and intelligent young men who helped to give the Conservative Party a more modern and vigorous image. He held a junior ministerial post under the Premiership of Sir Alec Douglas-Home. His special interest is in education and the problems of youth. He is highly literate and became a good broadcaster, especially on television. Since memories are short, this has probably been a greater aid to his political career than his former distinction at running.

In 1967, when the Greater London Council was won by the Conservatives after a very long period of Labour rule, he was co-opted as Chairman of the Education Committee, a function comparable with that of a Minister for Education in a fair-sized country. It is complicated by the fact that the national Government is the Labour Party which holds different views on education from the Conservatives, especially about secondary education. Chataway thus ran into cross-fire between his own Party and the Government. His own view, which he has expressed both privately and in public, is that education should be free from doctrinaire influences. He takes the practical view that the great need is for good schools, rather than for some particular form of school, such as the Comprehensive secondary school, which may be more egalitarian but will not necessarily be more efficient. He also considered that, as a question of priority, the Primary schools under his jurisdiction more urgently needed the available resources.

The solution he evolved – a compromise between a full comprehensive system and the retention of all traditional higher secondary schools – pleased neither of the committed bodies of opinion, but a man who could find the extra yards to beat Kuts and the world 5,000 metres record is not likely to be dismayed by opposition.

In his training Chataway enjoyed, as we have seen, the advantage of working at Oxford and elsewhere with a group of other distinguished and thoughtful athletes, and, after 1952, the advice of that most intelligent of coaches, Franz Stampfl. Nevertheless,

I

he was an individualist, as all great athletes must be. He has confessed that he cannot work up much enthusiasm for team competition. He was always glad if he found out later, after a complicated adding up of points for winners, seconds and thirds, that his team had won, but on the day (and often for some days before) he could think about nothing but his own individual struggle into which he had to put everything.

It is unfortunate that in athletic team competition (apart from Cross-country races) no one has yet thought up a satisfactory system of scoring in which the spectators can participate. In football, the progress of the game is obvious to all from goals scored. Cricket has its built-in statistical drama, from the relation between runs and wickets. There may be dreary periods when the cricket is negative, but as soon as it comes to life, the tension is immediately obvious to every spectator, and equally to every competitor in both teams. In athletics, the totting up of points for places, especially in long-drawn-out throwing and jumping events, destroys the drama which spectators want. They can get it only from the individual, immediate contests on the track, to which the statistics of team competition are not directly relevant. So the drama is naturally reflected in the attitudes of the competitors, and most of all to the longer distance races.

However strong their local or national patriotisms may be, the champions – that is, those who are in with a chance of winning – are bound to be obsessed with their own individual contest. Most of them are also good clubmen, but on the track in a major contest they are utterly alone right up to the finishing-post. In formulating this view, Chataway was simply putting his finger on the nature of athletics, the contest for the prize.

The latest in this line of succession, Ronald Clarke, is also a good clubman who enjoys training and competing locally with his friends. Equally, he is an individualist when he steps on the track. He has emerged as the most devastating runner to date at from 3 miles to 10,000 metres. He is taller and more powerful than the other champions discussed here, and stands out in a normal field of distance runners. This strong stature and the powerful stride give him an air of inevitability. At the Tokyo Olympic Games in 1964 he was not quite ready. He did everything he could in the 10,000 metres to break down Mills and Gammoudi, but just failed. They could not match the world record Clarke had set up 10 months before, but they held off his challenge.

Since then, he has been beaten twice, at 3 miles and 5,000 metres, by Keino, but – although he is the last man to make excuses – it is a fact that, the first time, he agreed to run at short notice, insufficiently prepared, and the second time he was hampered by a groin injury which noticeably shortened his stride towards the end of the race. Clarke was hoping to have a third race with Keino in London in July 1967 when he defended his 3 miles title at the AAA championships, but Keino was obliged to withdraw for political reasons which did not concern the main stream of international competition. Otherwise, Clarke has been unbeatable at his distances, and for the last 3 years his main task has been cutting down his own records.

In December 1963 in Melbourne he broke the record for 10,000 metres, set up by Bolotnikov in Moscow in August 1962, which had broken that of Kuts dating back to 1956, which again broke Zatopek's of 1954. The drive which Clarke has put into this form of running can be expressed in figures: Zatopek in 1954 ran the distance in 28 mins 54.2 secs; Kuts in 1956 brought this down to 28 mins 30.4 secs; Bolotnikov to 28 mins 18.2 secs. Ron Clarke in 1963 reduced it to 28 mins 15.6 secs. He could not improve on this in the year of the Tokyo Olympics, but the following year he got it down to 27 mins 39.4 secs. This meant that, other things being equal, Clarke would have beaten Zatopek by over a lap, Kuts by about 400 yards, and Bolotnikov by about 300. Mills and Gammoudi on their Tokyo form would have been about half way between Bolotnikov and Kuts. The relativities would be similar in the 5,000 metres.

Clarke manages to combine a heavy schedule of running with a successful career. By neglecting his athletics for a period he was able to qualify as an accountant and build up a business at which he works hard. He can find time to train hard and he takes an extended holiday about once a year to tour the world in search of top-class competition. He also has a satisfying family life.

As a basis, Clarke has a very strong physique and immense physical and mental energy. He is capable of running a race faster than anyone else can and then, appearing fresh and alert from the changing-room, spending an evening in intense discussion of half a dozen subjects thrown at him by half a dozen people. He has the hair-trigger memory and the swift power of decision of a high-power executive. Physical and mental concentration are matched. On the track he looks more relaxed than most athletes: there must be some tension, but he does not show it. Off the track he is completely relaxed, and pleasantly extrovert. He will talk to anyone about anything, including – but not for preference – himself.

He believes that athletic performance consists of 'training plus psychology'. By this he means that no one in this day and age can get far without a basis of rigorous training, but beyond that his performance will depend on his psychological approach – the amount of will-power and self-confidence he can muster, to break through a barrier which others consider unassailable. When he is asked what are the proportions (as Napoleon, for instance, said that the moral is to the material as 4 to 1) the shrewd executive comes uppermost, and he refuses to offer a judgment which would imply any specialist knowledge of psychology. But he is sure that George, Nurmi or Zatopek could have run faster if the target had been moved progressively further away. He therefore believes that there was and still is great scope for improvement of performance in the longer distances.

Clarke has been disappointed at the performance of British distance runners, many of whom have greater potential than they have exploited. He believes that they should both train and run more imaginatively than they do, by intensifying interval training, learning to vary their bursts of speed, experimenting in races, and above all choosing front running instead of the 'soft option' of tactical running. He does not like opponents who 'cling' in the hope of winning with a short finishing burst, and this dislike (which is not personal) makes him all the more ruthless in shaking them off.

This criticism puts a finger on the difference between the superlative runner and the excellent runner, which becomes more important as standards rise. The key word is 'imaginative' and by that Clarke means, first a high level of intelligence and secondly the intense application of this to the problems of competition. This is not much different from what Zatopek originally did, and what he expressed as 'the moral plus in sport'.

Clarke claims that he really enjoys running and will go on running as long as he enjoys it, irrespective of whether he is holding his place at the top of the table. It is difficult to imagine anyone actively enjoying the sensation of running as hard as Clarke does. Chataway admits quite frankly that the actual race is 'agony' when it approaches world record level, and most people would compare the pleasure with that of the lunatic who was alleged to keep hitting himself on the head with a hammer because he felt so good when he stopped. But Chataway was less systematically conditioned to fatigue, and Clarke finds that he can accept the discomfort in the excitement of imaginative concentration on the supreme effort. He has succeeded in creating a *modus vivendi* in which, however intensively he competes, he can fit his running into a full life and in this sense can claim that it is a hobby. At the same time, his motive in pursuing that sport was simply that he found he could do it better than anything else – and eventually anyone else. He would just as soon have been a top-class footballer if his talent had lain there.

Finally, there is that most remarkable phenomenon, Abebe Bikila of Ethiopia, who has never competed seriously on the track (fortunately for the 10,000 metres champions) but is unapproachable over the Marathon distance. Addis Ababa is rather far to travel for an interview, but a friend and colleague, Berhanu Tibebu of the *Ethiopian Herald*, who knows Bikila well, has conducted an interview with him for the purpose of this book, and this is what he writes:

What is the influence of age on long-distance running? Lt. Abebe Bikila, two-time marathon winner in Rome and Tokyo, says: 'If you keep yourself in good shape, you can never be too old for the Olympics.'

Abebe Bikila is now 35. When he competes in the Olympics to be held in Mexico, he will be 36. Despite the 4 years between the Tokyo and the Mexico Olympic events, Bikila is confident that he will win for the third time, and even believes that he will stand a good chance at the age of 40.

Bikila believes that a marathon runner need not be lacking strength to compete at top level after the age of 35. Constant practice makes the athlete's body grow stronger and stronger. His muscles become more and more flexible and better attuned to the competition. He may not be in a better position to break

records than at an earlier age, but Bikila believes that the body
well strengthened through constant practice greatly contributes
to the athlete's chance of winning the Olympics.

Lt. Bikila is the first long-distance runner in the history of
the Olympics to win two marathon gold medals consecutively,
or, indeed, at all. His Rome record in 1960 was 2 hrs 15 mins
16.2 secs. His Tokyo record in 1964 was less by 3 mins and 5
secs. In Rome, at 29 years of age, Bikila ran and won the marathon race barefooted.

In September 1967 Bikila had his 35th birthday. He has high
hopes of winning the marathon at 36 in the Mexico Olympics.
He weighs 58 kilos and measures 1.75 metres.* As compared to
other athletes, he has a slim bodily make-up, a type of body
that seems to be built for long-distance running. He is a self-
composed man full of energy and tenacity. His face expresses
determination and confidence. Pleasant to talk with, he is well
versed in giving illustrations of what he discusses by using
witticisms and proverbs. He is neither aggressive nor shy. He
seems to be a man in full control of his bodily and mental
faculties.

When he competes, he runs at a regular, even pace always
sure of reaching his goal. He does not run for personal prestige.
He says he loves running and that he is very much interested
in it. He aims at beating his opponents first, as he says, to keep
up the name of his country, and then at breaking his own
record to see by how much he can improve over his previous
achievement.

Bikila told me that he relies purely on methods he himself
has evolved in the various competitions in which he has participated during the past 7 years, and that he does not owe
anything to any athlete. As for the advice of a coach, he
seriously pays attention to it, but adds that he greatly depends
on his own methods and judgment.

Among the marathon runners for whom he has admiration,
Bikila mentions the Moroccan marathon runner Rhadi.† Rhadi
competed with Bikila in the Rome Olympics and came out
second within a distance of some 500 metres. He also mentioned
the name of his own countryman, Mamo Wolde. This man has

---

* 9 stones 2 pounds and 5 feet 10 inches.
† Abdesselem.

earned quite a name in long-distance running and has won several international competitions in Europe outside the Olympics. Bikila believes that, with greater effort and encouragement, Mamo Wolde will show a remarkable result in Olympic competition.

Bikila was born in the countryside, near Addis Ababa, the capital city. During his early days, Bikila recalls that he used to love playing 'gugs' – a game of horsemanship – and 'Gena – a hockey type of game played among villages. The latter game demands some skills in running, and unlike hockey, there are no goal-posts as such, and any side makes a score when he takes the ball to a point regarded as the farthest end of the opponent's position, as agreed by the two parties. The game thus requires a lot of running about on the part of the players.

Although Bikila rarely plays 'Gena' today, he still loves riding horses. This is not because riding adds anything to his skill in the marathon race, but simply because he loves riding as a pastime. But what he regards as most essential for the marathon race is physical exercise. Before he starts any training session, he does gymnastics. It is well remembered, for example, that Bikila surprised spectators at the Tokyo Olympics when, after finishing off his race, he proceeded to do some physical exercises.

Physical exercises after a marathon race, when several competitors fall by the way fainting, is indeed a great feat to accomplish. It appears as if it is something that the human body cannot endure. But for Bikila, whether at the beginning or at the end, physical exercise is a 'must'. He is extremely disciplined; and it is partly due to this and his innate strength of character that he achieves what most of us regard as an inestimable feat.

In this report, Mr Tibebu stresses Bikila's strength of character – which no one could doubt in a marathon-runner – but it is equally clear that Bikila has also brought great intelligence and inventiveness to his running. He thus fits into the general pattern of the superlative runners dealt with in this chapter.

All these athletes are (or were) imaginative in the sense Ron Clarke means it. They applied their intelligence to the problems of training and competition in an original way based partly on their own thinking and what they could learn from others, and partly on persistent experiment. They were all formidably ruthless on the track and amiable off it. None suffered from the inflation of the ego which is often found in other sports, yet they were all individualistic and strong-minded. It goes without saying that they were all endowed with exceptional physiques, especially in the complicated metabolism required for rapid oxygen-recovery. But most important of all are the moral attributes: intelligence, independence of mind and strength of character.

9

The Means and the Ends

In June 1886 the Lillie Bridge ground in Fulham came to a sad end. It had been opened in 1869 as the second stadium in Britain, in Europe, and probably the world, with a cinder-track (called in those days a cinder-path). There was already a cinder-track at Beaufort House in London, where the first Amateur Athletic Club championships were held in 1866, but Lillie Bridge became the leading ground from 1869. It had a 440-yard track laid down on a foundation of bricks and stones, covered with a surface of cinders from one of the many gas-processing plants in London which yielded coke or cinders as a by-product. Within the next 10 years, several cinder-tracks were laid in the United States, but the Lillie Bridge track, as far as recorded history goes, was the first of its kind to be widely used for athletic competition.

It was adopted by the Amateur Athletic Club of Great Britain in 1869 for their British championships. The cinder-track was superior to the grass-tracks which had hitherto been used, because the porous cinder covering, several inches deep, allowed rain to run off or sink in, whereas turf, although very fast when dry, became bogged by heavy or continuous rain. In 1877 another cinder-track was laid down less than a mile away from Lillie Bridge, at Stamford Bridge, where the Chelsea professional Football Club now plays its matches.

Both grounds were actually in Fulham, but because there was already a Fulham Football Club, in a ground about equidistant from Lillie Bridge and Stamford Bridge, the newer football club, which was on the Chelsea side of Fulham, called itself Chelsea. Its cinder-track survived until 1931, and was used till then for all major athletic contests, including the AAA Championships.

By then the directors of the Chelsea Football Club had taken to hiring out the track to 'dirt-track' motor-cycling racing promoters, and the deterioration of the track was so noticeable by 1930, that the Amateur Athletic Association decided to move to the White City Stadium, near Shepherd's Bush, where athletes share a rather second-rate track with greyhounds, who operate on a fast grass-track outside the cinder-track, with considerable profit to the promoters of dog-racing.

The Lillie Bridge ground, which had the best running-track London has ever had, was destroyed in 1886. After the Amateur Athletic Club was supplanted by the AAA, which plumped for the nearby Stamford Bridge Ground, because the London Athletic Club which used it had defeated the AAC in the struggle for power, the Lillie Bridge ground was thrown open to private enterprise. The inside of the track was used as a football pitch, and some Football Association Cup Finals were played there in the seventies. The track was used for professional running. In 1885, George defeated Cummings there in his classic race in which he put the world mile record at 4 mins 12¾ secs, where it stayed until Nurmi reduced it 48 years later.

Unfortunately, the Lillie Bridge ground went out of business in 1886. A professional race was arranged at 100 yards between two famous sprinters, Gent and Hutchins. Harry Hutchins, despite a formidable moustache which must have created some wind-resistance, was reputed to be the 'fastest thing on 2 legs'. He was credited in the early eighties with 30 seconds for 300 yards. On this occasion – no doubt for a perfectly good reason: he was an honest professional – Hutchins failed to turn up, and Gent ran over the course to win in a 'walk-over'. He then claimed the stake-money, for which he and Hutchins were to have contended. The crowd of about 30,000 spectators, who mostly had expected Hutchins to win, felt cheated of its competition, and perhaps also of the bets placed on Hutchins, and rioted. They pulled down the wooden fencing and made a bonfire of it, also destroying the dressing-rooms and grandstand.

The Lillie Bridge ground never recovered from this outbreak of vandalism. It remained derelict for a couple of years and then was sold to the Great Western Railway, which has since used it as a marshalling yard.

By then there were at least 5 other cinder-tracks in England:

2 in London, and 1 each at Oxford, Cambridge and Birmingham, and more than that number in the United States, where facilities were being developed much faster.

At the end of the century, Charles H. Sherill, one time Captain of Yale, whose remarks on American training methods have been quoted,* described the contrast between English and American facilities. He wrote: †

'The writer well remembers his experience when he first went to London, a number of years ago, and tried to find the club-house of the London Athletic Club. After huge sums of British gold had been expended by him in fruitless cab voyages, he finally arrived at Stamford Bridge Grounds, and found the club-house – underneath the grandstand! Almost every athletic club of any importance in our country has a comfortable club-house. The comforts and size of these club-houses vary as the strength of the clubs, until finally we reach the huge palaces owned by the New York Athletic Club, the Chicago Athletic Association, Boston Athletic Association, the Athletic Club of Philadelphia, the Columbia Athletic Club of Washington, and others too numerous to mention. At the date of this writing the New York Athletic Club is just moving into its new club-house, which has cost over two million dollars; it is completely fitted out with reading rooms, billiard rooms, dining rooms, Russian and Turkish baths; a huge marble-lined swimming tank; a spacious gymnasium, occupying the top floor of the building in order to secure for it the best possible light; boxing room, wrestling room, fencing room, numerous sleeping apartments, roof garden overlooking Central Park, etc. In addition to this beautiful house, this greatest of all athletic clubs has a charming country house on Tavern Island on the Sound. This ideal spot, beautiful by nature, has been beautified by art. The one-fifth of a mile track lies in a snug little hollow enclosed by gracefully sloping grassy banks. Every comfort that an athlete could wish is to be found there, including a large country house capable of accommodating 300 members, with ample sleeping apartments, numerous tennis courts, baseball and football fields, a large boathouse stocked with numerous shells‡ and other aquatic gear, a yacht-house where the yachting members may stow their tackle during the non-commission days of winter, etc. To this

* Chapter II, p. 38.
† *Athletics*, by Montague Shearman, Longman's Green & Co., 1898.
‡ i.e. sculling-boats.

athletic paradise, when the heat of summer makes the city unbearable, one may creep away and take his recreation in such form of gentle or lively exercise as may suit him best, in the company of many a newly fledged and many an old-time athlete, where the abundance of recreation will more than amply compensate him for the possible absence of *otium cum dignitate.** Here are held the club's spring and autumn games, to which one may come by invitation only, as no tickets are sold.'

When Continental countries took up organised athletic competition after about 1890, they also created better facilities than British athletes have ever enjoyed. Clubs tended to be, like the New York Athletic Club, multi-purpose. The athletics section was only one branch, and most clubs had a football pitch, tennis courts and other facilities, which all helped to finance the operation. State and municipal help was given because sporting activities were obviously of social benefit, and tracks and facilities for field events were generally of a much higher standard than in Britain, where an extreme puritanism, originating in the fear of contamination by professionalism, has remained to this day.

There was a period after 1945 when athletics became very popular in Britain, and it was easy to attract 30,000 spectators to major events. The AAA could have prospered, with a little business-like management. Unfortunately, this was lacking, and athletics in Britain has sunk back into an aura of shabby-gentility. It was depressing at the AAA Championships in 1963 to see that magnificent American Pole-vaulter, J. T. Pennell, in setting up an all-comers' and world record, just failing to clear 17 feet through defective facilities. The run-up to the pole-vault at the White City is so short that Pennell had to start his run on the track, and was constantly interrupted by runners in the track races. That he achieved 16 ft. 10¼ in. (5.14 metres), still the best performance in Great Britain, was a tremendous tribute to his power of concentration, but the conditions under which he was obliged to compete were a disgrace to British athletics.

In almost every athletics match between Britain and an American or Continental team, the field events points are a write-off

* (Dignified leisure) the contemporary New York term used to satirise aesthetes or 'Greenery-gallery'.

for Britain, mainly because the British athletics authorities do not provide adequate facilities for these events and do not know how to present them at sports meetings in a way which could catch the public imagination. The one exception is in the long-jump, and it is not a coincidence that the British and Olympic champion, Lynn Davies, is a lecturer in Physical Education who can create his own training environment, for himself as well as his students.

In long-distance running, sophisticated facilities are not important. Much of the strength of British running is based on cross-country, which needs no preparation. Track performances in Britain tend to be slower than elsewhere, because the big meetings are held on inferior tracks. That runners like Nurmi, Chataway, Kuts and Clarke have managed to break records on British tracks is a tribute to their power of overcoming any obstacle, but if they want to tackle a record in which every second counts, they go to Helsinki, Turku, Prague, Kiev or Los Angeles.

The latest development which concerns long-distance runners is the 'Tartan' track. This is an all-weather rubber surface, which gives complete reliability and great spring. It enables runners to run faster than on normal tracks, just as some American indoor boarded and banked tracks have since the last century produced faster performances than any outdoor cinder-track. The AAA and British Olympic Committee decided in their wisdom that it would be 'uneconomic' to lay down a Tartan track in Britain, because it would not be used enough times in the year to amortise the capital outlay. They have laid down a small strip for practice purposes, which enables sprinters to try it out, but is no use to distance-runners.*

The first result of this innovation, as far as British runners were concerned, was that McCafferty, the only distance-runner in the modest team of 8 athletes† sent over to compete in the pre-liminary trial of the Mexico City facilities, the so-called 'Little Olympics' held in October, 1967, failed to qualify for the final of the 5,000 metres, which he might well have won. McCafferty was not worried by the altitude: he found that he could not run as

---

* Since this was written, the Greater London Council has agreed to subsidise a full Tartan track in the London area.
† The AAA could not raise the money for more than 4, but the BBC paid for the rest.

fast as at sea-level, but that by starting slowly and increasing his pace in the second-half of the race he could run away from the field. This he did, but at the beginning of the last lap he was seized with cramp owing to the unaccustomed Tartan surface. He stopped and took his shoes off, was overtaken by the other runners, then courageously finished the last lap in great pain, but just failed to qualify for the final.

Meanwhile American athletes who can get themselves accustomed to the Tartan track surface, have been able to improve their performance. This is the first revolutionary development in long-distance running facilities since the cinder-track a century ago. When properly utilised at sea-level it could be worth as much as 20 seconds in 5,000 metres. Taken together with the advantage of altitude-training, it should bring the 5,000 metres record down to about 12 mins 40 secs within the next couple of years, and the 3 miles to inside 12 mins 20 secs, or about 4 mins 6 secs a mile. British athletes will not share these benefits (unless they can study at American Universities) but there is no reason why Ron Clarke – if he can take a couple of months off from his business – or Keino, or Jim Ryun, when he moves upwards from the mile, or Norpoth, Gammoudi, Lindgren or Jazy, should not reach this standard.

In ancient Greece, the track was of sun-baked powdery earth, and dust is constantly mentioned in the context of athletics, as when Milton wrote in his immortal lines in 'Areopagitica': 'I cannot praise a fugitive and cloistered virtue, unexercised and un-breathed, that never sallies out and sees his adversary, but slinks out of the battle when that immortal garland is to be run for, not without dust and heat.' The dust-clouds often made life difficult for the judges, and they favoured the front-runner, who blinded his pursuer with his slip-stream, unless – like Odysseus in his race with Ajax as Homer describes it – the pursuer could stay close enough to breathe down the front-runner's neck.* Grass and cinders eliminated the dust factor, and now the Tartan track combines the best features of both: grass in perfect condition is faster than cinders, but cinders resist rain better. The Tartan is springier than the best turf and more weather-resistant than cinders.

Thus runners now have their perfect environment (if officials

* Chapter I, p. 15.

can be persuaded to provide it) which corresponds to the greatly improved run-ups and take-offs for the jumps, and the fibre-glass poles for vaulting, which give the maximum lift at the moment of truth.

These improved means will improve performance, but the great beauty of distance-running is that it relies so little on the amenities. Bikila ran bare-footed on the road in his epoch-making marathon at Rome. Roger Bannister always sharpened his spikes before a major race, but it is doubtful whether that gained him $\frac{1}{10}$ of a second – apart from the psychological comfort it gave him.

Another big advance in recent years has been the development of expert coaching. In earlier times there were trainers or 'rubbers' who gave athletes help mainly in massage and the sort of facilities provided by a second in the corner of the boxing ring between rounds. This was a very old tradition: the Greeks were great believers in massage. They had themselves thoroughly rubbed with olive-oil and powdered with dust. When athletics revived in 19th Century Britain, the trainer-masseur was a *sine-qua-non*. Most athletes still remember, as their first impression of competition, the smell of oil of wintergreen which was a traditional component of all embrocations for men and horses, and pervaded all changing-rooms. At the Oxford University Athletic Club in the twenties and thirties of this century there was a splendid character called Jack the Rubber, who would massage the limbs of members and put iodine on their abrasions, keeping up their morale with an unceasing monologue in good Yorkshire.

Massage is undoubtedly of great value in keeping the limbs supple and preventing muscular strains. Without it, the muscular fibres are apt to tear under sudden strain, especially in cold weather, and this produces the painful disability usually called a 'pulled muscle'.

There is, however, now a more sophisticated form of help to athletes, originally developed in the United States, the Coach. This is a man who may or may not have been a first-class athlete himself, but who takes a thoughtful interest in the techniques of running and field events and is able to teach athletes how to improve their performances. They usually set up as consultants and gather a few pupils round them. Sam Mussabini, who coached Albert Hill, Harold Abrahams and other distinguished

British athletes just after the 1st World War, was one of the earliest in Europe.

They began writing text-books about their methods. One, Woldemar Gerschler, in Nazi Germany produced the first considered exposition of interval training in a book published in 1939, although owing to the War it did not make an impact at the time. There were also a number of Scandinavians who have already been mentioned, including Gosta Olander and Henry Kalarne, who introduced the 'Fartlek' method in Sweden.

Now every country has official coaches, and most athletes get instruction at some stage. The AAA has an excellent network headed by John Le Masurier, which is especially active among young athletes. Two of the most distinguished contemporary coaches, who both operate in Australia, exemplify two distinct schools of thought. Percy Wells Cerutty, who runs a training establishment at Portsea, Victoria, believes in 'owning' his pupils, body and soul, and preaching at them a philosophy which he has derived from the Gospels and other popular sources. He has written a good deal, but his books do not, in my view, communicate his undoubtedly successful methods. There is nothing revolutionary about Cerutty's system, which includes 'Fartlek', interval training and weight-lifting exercises: all well-worn themes. He seems to rely on a psychological approach based on a mixture of revivalism and high-pressure salesmanship.

Another Australian, of Austrian origin, Franz Stampfl, represents the opposite approach. He believes in letting his pupils work out their own destiny, and confining himself to advice and encouragement. A number of very distinguished athletes, including Bannister, Chataway, Mervyn Lincoln and Clarke, who all in principle prefer to work out their own methods, have nevertheless benefited from Stampfl's advice.

Chataway in particular said that when he first met Stampfl, he had been seriously considering giving up top-class competition, but he found Stampfl's enthusiasm so infectious that he changed his mind, and afterwards found Stampfl's advice extremely valuable. Stampfl is thus the most adult type of coach who can convey most to the more intelligent type of athlete. He has written an extremely intelligent book* to which Chataway contributed a preface in which he wrote: 'That I ran better than ever before in the

* *Franz Stampfl on Running*, Herbert Jenkins, 1955.

No expense spared: the New York Athletic Club Town House in 1896

Jim Ryun strikes: Emsley Carr International Mile race, London 1967

season that followed, I attribute in large measure to Franz Stampfl. That I enjoyed running more than ever before was, I am sure, almost entirely due to him.'

Nevertheless, whatever improvements there have been in tracks and in coaching, the long-distance runner is still very much alone when he walks on to the track. What he achieves finally all comes out of himself: from the training schedule he has operated, his determination to win, and the intelligence and fortitude he applies to the race. His disciplines are the most simple and the most severe of all. Therein lies the splendour and the fascination of long-distance running.

K

APPENDIX:

Olympic Facts and Figures

(I) *Development*

In this book the term 'Olympiad' has been given its current usage in most European languages, including English, as one of the 4-yearly Olympic festivals of Games since their revival in 1896. Its meaning in Greek was the 4-year period between one Olympic Festival and another. This chronological cycle dated traditionally from 776 BC and for calendrical purposes it was described under the name of the winner of the foot-race at the Festival from which it began. Thus, the period from July 765 BC, to June 764 BC, would be categorised as the 2nd Year of the Olympiad of Coroebus (the Champion in 776).

The modern Olympics, started at Athens in April, 1896, are also held at 4-year intervals and, although 'Olympiad' is used to mean the actual competition or festival, not the time-span, the organisers still defer to ancient Greek custom by numbering the Olympiads as 4-yearly periods, beginning from 1896, whether or not they are actually celebrated. They are therefore, in their Charter, using the term in its Greek sense, although Olympiads do not figure in leasehold agreements, or peace treaties, as they did in Ancient Greece, and no one else now uses the term in that sense. For this reason, the Olympic Games which start in Mexico City in October 1968 will be the XIX Olympiad, although it is actually the 16th Olympic Games of the modern sort, because the VI Olympiad, which would have been held in Berlin in 1916, was a non-event owing to the First World War, and the XII and XIII Olympiads, planned for 1940 and 1944, were cancelled because of the Second World War. This shows that we are more businesslike about war these days: in Ancient Greece the Olympics were celebrated for some 1,200 years, and when there was a conflict of interest between war-lords and Olympic organisers, it was the war that was called off.

The first modern Games in Athens were held in a stadium which was a replica of the original Olympic stadium. They were sparsely attended, and performances were of a low standard, partly because the athletes were unrepresentative, and partly because facilities were poor. The track was only about 30 yards across, so that runners had impossibly sharp bends to negotiate. The 400 metres was won in 54.2 secs (although Tyndall of Great Britain had set up a world record of 48.5 secs 7 years before). The 800 metres was won in 2 mins 11 secs, compared with the existing world record of Kilpatrick of the United States of 1 min 53.4 secs, for the slightly longer distance of 880 yards. The 1,500 metres took 4 mins 33.2 secs. Contests were also held in jumping, throwing, cycling, fencing, shooting, lawn-tennis, gymnastics and weight-lifting. The marathon, run on the last day, stole the show, and has ever since been the last event and climax of Olympiads.

The 2nd and 3rd Olympiads, in Paris and St Louis, aroused little interest. The Games really took off with the IV Olympiad in London in 1908, when a climate of international competition had begun to develop. The pattern was set for future Olympics.

The V Olympiad at Stockholm in 1912 was also successful and helped to consolidate the Games as a genuinely world event. VI Olympiad, 1916, was not contested. VII was in Antwerp, 1920, VIII again in Paris, 1924, and IX was Amsterdam, 1928. X in Los Angeles, 1932, was the most lavish and highly contested to date, but XI in Berlin, 1936, outdid even America and set the pattern of using Olympic festivals as adjuncts to the build-up of national prestige and the tourist trade. The Nazis also introduced a considerable political and ideological factor, which fortunately has been avoided since then. The Second World War washed out XII and XIII Olympiads, and it was left to war-weary Britain to restore the image of normality. This job was well done at the Wembley Games of 1948, and it is not always recognised that a good deal was owed to the British Broadcasting Corporation, which, apart from its expertise in sports-reporting, had built up a powerful overseas broadcasting network during the War, and used this adeptly to broadcast reports and results and provide facilities for the broadcasting stations of other countries to report back home.

It was also fortunate that the XV Olympiad went to Helsinki in 1952, where the Finns, with their great tradition of athletics and athletic organisation, were able to put on an inspiring show. Since then, the Olympiads have reflected the post-war shrinkage of the globe: Melbourne in 1956, Rome in 1960, Tokyo in 1964, and now Mexico City.

(II) *Organisation*

The Games are run by the Olympic Committee (Comité International Olympique) with permanent Headquarters at Mon Repos, Lausanne, Switzerland. It consists normally of 72 members elected for life, not to represent their countries on the Committee, but to represent the Committee to their countries. No country is allowed more than 3 members and, since retirement is rare, the average age is high – something over 60.

The Committee is often described as a self-governing oligarchy, and its processes are anything but democratic. It does not publish accounts, agendas, or reports of its debates. Its composition is an odd mixture of aristocracy, plutocracy and State-nominated delegates from Communist member countries (7 in number). Committee members also include a King, a Rajah, a Sheik, a Grand Duke and 2 Princes. Yet the Committee manages to get on amicably and to run the Olympic Games efficiently and fairly, and to keep them reasonably free of political and nationalist pressures. This is due partly to the fact that most members are genuinely independent of their Governments. The 7 Communist members often vote *en bloc*, but otherwise there are none of the alignments and lobbies which characterise the United Nations and other international bodies. As the Committee meets only once every 3 months, the President, who has a permanent secretariat, exercises great influence.

The first President was the Baron Coubertin himself, who retired in 1925 (he died in 1937). He was succeeded by a Belgian aristocrat, Count Henry de Baillet Latour, who died in 1942. A Swedish gentleman, J. Sigfrid Edstrom, steered the Committee through its post-war reconstruction. In 1952 he was succeeded by a wealthy American, Avery Brundage, who is now 80, and has been as determined to maintain the purity of Olympic competition as ever Baron de Coubertin was. He has had to deal with the endemic pressures of national interests and intensive lobbying for the privilege of staging the Games (the decision is normally made at least 5 years in advance). Because of its diverse and individual structure, the Committee is better able to resist outside lobbying than most organisations.

The Charter of the Olympic Games lists the following fundamental principles:

1) The Olympic Games are celebrated every 4 years. They assemble the AMATEURS of all nations on an equal footing and under conditions as perfect as possible.

2) An Olympiad need not be celebrated but neither the order nor the intervals can be altered. The International Olympiads are counted as beginning from the 1st Olympiad of the modern era, celebrated at Athens in 1896.

3) The International Olympic Committee has the sole right to choose the place for the celebration of each Olympiad.

4) The Olympic Games must include the following events: Athletics, Gymnastics, Combative Sports, Swimming, Equestrian Sports, Pentathlon and Art Competitions.

5) There is a distinct cycle of Olympic Winter Games which are celebrated in the same year as the other Games.

Starting from the 8th Olympiad, they take the title of the First Olympic Winter Games but the term Olympiad will not be used to describe them.

6) The International Olympic Committee chooses the place for the celebration of the Olympic Winter Games, giving the first refusal to the country holding the current Olympic Games on condition that it can give sufficient guarantees to organize the full programme of the Winter Games.

7) Generally speaking, only those who are natives of a country or naturalized subjects of that country are qualified to compete in the Olympic Games under the colours of that country.

(III) *Programme and Performance*

The festivals have grown progressively bigger and more elaborate. The Athletics events at Athens were: 100 metres, 400 metres, 800 metres, 1,500 metres, Marathon, 110 metres hurdles, High Jump, Pole Vault, Long Jump, Hop Step and Jump (Triple Jump), Putting the Shot and Discus. In 1900 there were added: 200 metres, 400 metres hurdles, and Hammer-throw. In 1908 Throwing the Javelin was started, and in 1912 the important additions were made of the 5,000 metres, 10,000 metres, Decathlon and relays of 4 by 100 metres and 4 by 400. In 1920 the 3,000 metres Steeplechase was introduced, in 1932 a 50,000 metres Walk and in 1956 a 20,000 metres Walk, bringing the Programme to its present state.

There had also been some events which did not survive: a tug of war, standing jumps, 60 metres sprint, 5 Miles Race, Cross-country individual and team races, a 3 Miles Team Race and shorter walking races at about 2 miles, which caused so much animosity owing to differing views on fair action that they were dropped.

The following list gives the present holders (i.e. gold medallists at Tokyo, 1964) with their performances, Olympic Record and World Record (as at December 1967). An asterisk in the middle column signifies that the Olympic record is held by the athlete shown in the left-hand column with his Tokyo performance. Distance of jumps and throws are shown in metres and decimal points of metres joined by an 'equal' sign to the equivalent in feet and inches.

Event	Holder		Olympic Record	World Record
100 m.	R. Hayes (US)	10 secs.	*	10 secs. Hayes, Hary (Ger.), Jerome. (Can.), H. Estevez (Venezuela), Chen Chia-chuan (China)
200 m.	H. Carr (US)	20.3 secs.	*	19.9 secs. Tommie Smith (US)
400 m.	M. Larrabee (US)	45.1 secs.	44.9 O. Davis (US) C. Kayfmann (Ger.)	44.6 secs. A. Plummer (US)
800 m.	P. Snell (NZ)	1:45.1	*	1:44.2 J. Ryun (US)
1500 m.	P. Snell	3:38.1	3:35.6 H. Elliott (Aus.)	3:33.1 J. Ryun (US)
5000 m.	R. Schul (US)	13:48.8	13:39.6 V. Kuts (USSR)	13:16.6 R. Clarke (Aus.)
10,000 m.	W. Mills (US)	28:24.4	*	27:39.4 R. Clarke (Aus.)
Steeplechase	G. Roelants (Bel.)	8:30.8	*	8:26.4 Roelants
Marathon	Abebe Bikila (Eth.)	2:12:11.2	*	Bikila
110 m. Hurdles	H. Jones (US)	13.6	13.5 L. Calhoun (Aus.)	13.2 M. Lauer (Ger.)
400 m. Hurdles	W. Cawley (US)	49.6	49.3 G. Davis (US)	49.0 G. Potgieter (SA)
High Jump	V. Brumel (SU)	2.18 m. = 7 ft. 1¼	*	2.28 m. = 7 ft. 5¼ Brumel
Long Jump	L. Davies (GB)	8.07 m. = 26 ft. 5¾	8.12 m. = 26 ft. 7¾ R. Boston (US)	8.35 m. = 27 ft. 5 Boston

Event	Holder	Olympic Record	World Record
Pole Vault	F. Hansen (US)	5.10 m. = 16 ft. 8¾	*	5.35 m. = 17 ft. 6¾ J. Pennell (US)
Triple Jump	J. Schmidt (Pol.)	16.85 m. = 55 ft. 3½	*	17.03 m. = 55 ft. 10¼ Schmidt
Shot	D. Long (US)	20.33 m. = 66 ft. 8½	*	21.52 m. = 70 ft. 7¼ R. Matson (US)
Discus	A. Oerter (US)	61.00 m. = 200 ft. 1½	*	66.07 m. = 216 ft. 9 L. Danek (CSR)
Hammer	R. Klim (SU)	69.74 m. = 228 ft. 10½	*	73.75 m. = 241 ft. 11½ G. Zsivotsky (Hung.)
Javelin	P. Nevala (Fin.)	82.66 m. = 271 ft. 2	85.71 m. = 281 ft. 2¼ E. Danielsen (Nor.)	91.72 m. = 300 ft. 11 T. Pedersen (Nor.)
Decathlon	W. Holdorf (Ger.)	7,887 pts.	8,001 R. Johnson (US)	8,234 W. Toomey (US)
4 × 100 m. Relay	USA	39.0 secs.	*	39.0 secs. USA
4 × 400 m. Relay	USA	3:00.7	*	2:59.6 USA
20 km. Walk	K. Matthews (GB)	1:29:34	*	1:28:01.8 H-J. Pathus (EG)
50 km. Walk	A. Pamich (Ital.)	4:11:12.4	*	4:06:22 G. Agapov (SU)

* The asterisk in the middle column signifies that the Olympic record is held by the athlete shown in the left hand column, with his Tokyo performance.

INDEX

Date Due